PUFFIN BOOKS

SCI-FI EXPLAINED:
TECHNO FUTURE

Herbie Brennan is the author of more than sixty books for children and adults, including the best-selling *Grailquest* series. His wife and he live in Ireland, where their lives are ruled by a cat called The Maggot.

W9-CFQ-906

Sci-Fi Explained:

Techno Future

Herbie Brennan

PUFFIN BOOKS

For Sam and Brian

PUFFIN BOOKS

Published by the Penguin Group
Penguin Books Ltd, 27 Wrights Lane, London W8 5TZ, England
Penguin Putnam Inc., 375 Hudson Street, New York, New York 10014, USA
Penguin Books Australia Ltd, Ringwood, Victoria, Australia
Penguin Books Canada Ltd, 10 Alcorn Avenue, Toronto, Ontario, Canada
M4V 3B2
Penguin Books (NZ) Ltd, Private Bag 102902, NSMC,
Auckland, New Zealand

On the World Wide Web at: www.penguin.com

Penguin Books Ltd, Registered Offices: Harmondsworth, Middlesex,
England

First published 2000
1 3 5 7 9 10 8 6 4 2

Text copyright © Herbie Brennan, 2000
Illustrations copyright © Jeff Anderson, 2000
Image p.9 supplied by Science & Society Picture Library
Photo p.20 supplied by Rex Features Limited
Photo p.36 supplied by Ronald Grant Archive
Photo p.41 © AFP Photo, supplied by P.A. News
Photo p.57 supplied by Ronald Grant Archive
Photo p.71 supplied by Ronald Grant Archive
Photo p.90 supplied by Ronald Grant Archive
All rights reserved

The moral right of the author and illustrator has been asserted
Set in Helvetica

Made and printed in England by Clays Ltd, St Ives plc
Except in the United States of America, this book is sold subject to the
condition that it shall not, by way of trade or otherwise, be lent, re-sold,
hired out, or otherwise circulated without the publisher's prior consent in
any form of binding or cover other than that in which it is published and
without a similar condition including this condition being imposed on the
subsequent purchaser

British Library Cataloguing in Publication Data
A CIP catalogue record for this book is available from the British Library

ISBN 0–141–30525–8

Contents

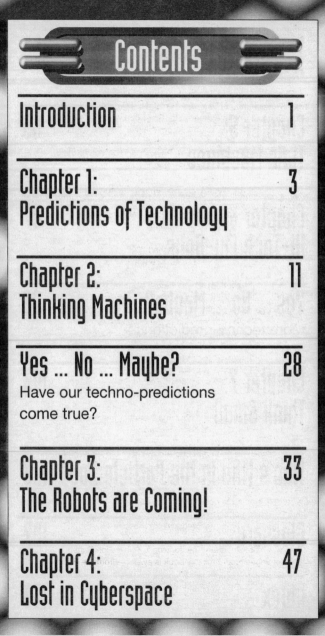

Introduction

Are you a sci-fi fan? Do you like watching movies or reading books whose subjects are space travel to the stars, future worlds, adventures through time, and weird inventions?

Science fiction is a lot of fun. Sci-fi authors can really let rip with their imagination when they write about what science will get up to next. But scientists themselves have to work with facts, with evidence, with hard reality. Unlike the writers, they can't just make things up. They look for rules – the laws of nature – that tell them how the universe works.

All the same, many scientists are sci-fi fans – and quite a few of them are sci-fi writers. In fact, some of them say that it was sci-fi that got them interested in science in the first place. That interest can last right through their lives. The world-famous physicist, Professor Stephen Hawking, himself appeared in *Star Trek: The Next Generation*, playing poker with Data and several other worthies.

The difference between science fiction and science fact can be far less than you might think – and that's one reason why so many scientists enjoy sci-fi. As you're about to find out, science-fiction writers can sometimes spot

1

genuine developments in science long before they come about.

There's a reason for this. Good science fiction isn't fantasy. Good science-fiction writers find out where science stands today before they try to see where it may be going tomorrow.

But the trouble is, science fact has recently been catching up with science fiction. Travel to the moon used to be science fiction . . . until Neil Armstrong did it for real. Death rays used to be science fiction . . . then somebody invented lasers. Even dear old television started out as science fiction, although it hasn't been science fiction for a very long time now.

In *Techno Future* you'll find out what the science-fiction writers predicted the technology of the future would be. More interestingly, you'll also find out where they got it right – and where they got it wrong.

But most interestingly of all, you're going to find out that the stuff the engineers and scientists are working on right now is often twice as weird as anything the sci-fi writers ever dreamed up.

Chapter 1

Predictions of Technology

Back in 1868, a Victorian futurologist made some calculations based on the most popular form of transport in those days, the covered carriage. He confidently predicted that by 1912, every street in London would be nearly two metres (six feet) deep in horse manure.

But in 1903 Henry Ford founded the Ford Motor Company. By 1912 the roads of Britain were filling up nicely with cars and there was not even a whiff of the manure crisis.

That's the trouble with predicting technology. You can't look at what you're using today and assume you'll just be using a rather better version of it tomorrow. Things don't work that way. Along comes some bright new invention and it's the prophets who end up six feet deep in horse manure.

Whoops!

Not that it stops them trying. The US Patent Office is the place in America where original ideas and inventions are registered. Its director, Charles H. Cuell, once urged the President of the United States to close it down because 'everything that can be invented has been invented'. This was back in 1899. In 1946, the chairman of IBM – now the largest computer company in the world – voiced the opinion that it was unlikely the world market for computers would ever be more than four machines.

The dividing line between prediction and science fiction has always been a little blurred. The Irish writer and churchman Jonathan Swift (1667–1745) penned a charming piece about men visiting the moon and he may well have been the first person ever to suggest such a thing. (At the time, the very idea of leaving our planet was extremely advanced, not to mention weird.) But did he really foresee the technology of Apollo 11 that produced the moon landing of 1969? Not quite. In Swift's story, the astronauts reached their destination in an open carriage drawn by geese.

Of course Swift didn't write science fiction as we think of it today. His works were a form of fantasy. The founding fathers of real science fiction were the Frenchman Jules Verne and the British writer, H. G. Wells. Their visions of the future were a mixture of accurate predictions and entertaining nonsense.

Herbert George Wells (1866–1946) was more interested in people than in science so that when, like Swift, he wrote about the first moon flight, it was based on the discovery of an imaginary substance called *cavourite* that screened out gravity – an idea today's scientists find almost as silly as a goose-drawn carriage.

Getting Better

Jules Verne (1828–1905) did better, probably because he took time to understand the science of his day. His books, written in the nineteenth century, contain descriptions of space flights, submarines, helicopters, air conditioning, guided missiles, and motion pictures, long before they were actually developed. The world's first atomic submarine, the *Nautilus*, was named after the craft in one of his most popular works, *20,000 Leagues under the Sea*.

Some of our present-day science-fiction writers manage to get it spot-on as well. One of the most famous of them, Arthur C. Clarke, penned a piece in which he suggested a great way to improve television communications.

TV waves travel in straight lines and so, because of the curvature of the Earth, tend to go shooting out into space once they've gone a certain distance. Clarke's idea was to put special satellites into orbit that would intercept the TV waves and bounce them back again over the curvature of the Earth so that the picture could be picked up in distant places.

What he was describing was the communications satellite, and he wrote the piece long before the first of them, *Telstar I*, was launched in 1962. He has since spent a lot of time kicking himself for not patenting the idea.

But even Arthur C. Clarke has nothing on the world's greatest prophet of future technology of all time, a man whose writings – and drawings – have stunned the scientific community. His name was Leonardo da Vinci.

Although art historians and others had known for a long time that Leonardo sometimes managed to describe inventions which didn't appear until centuries after his death, it wasn't until 1965 that people came to realize just how remarkable a prophet of technology he had really been. In that year, a series of texts written by Leonardo in his odd, backwards 'mirror writing' was discovered in Madrid, Spain.

These texts date from the late fifteenth century, yet they are packed with accurate, detailed descriptions of exploding missiles, modern machinery, streamlining and, most remarkable of all . . . a bicycle.

Bike Tech

The first step towards the development of the bicycle was the invention of the so-called 'hobby-horse', in France in the 1790s. Because the front wheel was fixed, it couldn't be steered; you just pushed it along with your feet on the ground. It wasn't until 1817 that a movable front wheel was introduced in Germany. In 1838, a Scottish blacksmith made the first bike with pedals which drove the rear wheel.

On the velocipede (a French invention of the 1860s) it was the front wheel that was pedal-driven, and the speed you could get up to depended on the size of the wheel – the bigger it was, the faster you went. The diameter of the front wheel of the penny-farthing – in use from the 1870s – got as big as one and a half metres (five feet) or more, while the back wheel was tiny, maybe a quarter that size. This made it very easy for the rider to fall off. A friend of mine ended up with forty-eight separate bruises after riding an antique penny-farthing for an hour.

The bicycle that appears in Leonardo's texts was actually far better designed than any of these models, despite the fact that the drawing was made 400 years earlier. It had equal-size wheels like a modern bicycle, a design feature that didn't appear again until J. K. Stanley's safety model in 1885. Even more amazing, Leonardo's version had pedals and a chain drive with gears to the back wheel, just like the bike you ride to school.

Guns and Bombs

Leonardo's texts also contain a sketch of what looks suspiciously like a modern guided missile. It had stabilizing fins and was nicely streamlined. Designed as a high-explosive artillery shell, it was years ahead of its time; it had two extra fins that jutted back from a pointed nose. The whole thing was to be stuffed with gunpowder which would explode when the shell struck something.

But the shell was only one of many hi-tech weapons described by Leonardo. Among others were shrapnel (not to be invented again until early in the nineteenth century), the breech-loading cannon, water-cooled gun-barrels, rocket-propelled grenades, and even a machine-gun!

And it didn't stop there! He described a wire-making device, a modern lathe, a wood planer with adjustable clamps, threaded nuts (the kind you use with bolts), a shearing machine to cut the nap off woollen cloth, and the world's first air-screw in the form of a roasting machine that used the hot air rising from the fire to turn the meat automatically.

The marvels go on and on. The manuscripts contain instructions for building flying machines (yes, flying machines), including a helicopter, for making release mechanisms that automatically drop a load when it is lowered to its fullest extent, for air- and water-turbines, for mechanical looms.

Somehow Leonardo managed to describe the modern method of copper engraving at a time when the printing press itself had only just been invented and the most advanced way of making an impression was by woodcuts. He

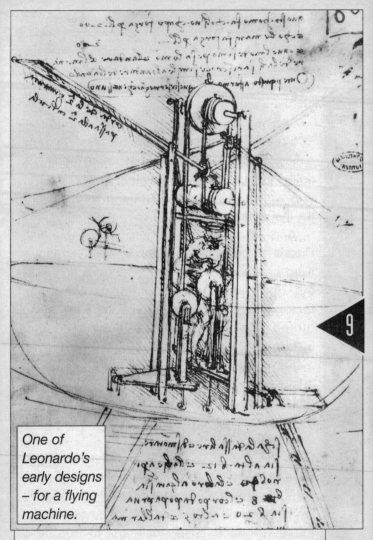

One of Leonardo's early designs – for a flying machine.

designed a simple camera . . . He sketched screws, keys, rivets, bearings, pins, axles, shafts, couplings, ropes, belts, chains, friction wheels, toothed wheels, flywheels, levers, connecting rods, click wheels, gears, ratchets, brakes, engaging and disengaging gearing, pipes, pistons, pump cylinders, valves, springs, cranks, cams and pulleys.

Not bad for a man born on 15 April 1452.

Finds like Leonardo's notebooks show how difficult it is to decide that what you're reading is actually science fiction. Was that what Leonardo was writing? Or was he just the greatest inventor the world has ever known?

And what do you make of people like Russia's Konstantin Tsiolkovsky and Germany's Kurd Lasswitz? Both were science-fiction writers. Both wrote books about space travel and rocketry long before these notions were being turned into reality on the drawing board. (Konstantin wrote in the 1920s, Kurd even earlier, in the late 1800s.) And both their books stimulated real scientists to get to work on ockets. So, did these two predict the future in their science fiction? Or did they actually help *create* it?

In the rest of this book we'll be looking at what happened to other science-fiction predictions, including many that concern themselves with the technology we're likely to develop in the future. In each case, we'll try to see how sen-sible the science in the fiction really is, how likely the predictions are to come true.

The space vessel, *Warp 9*, is travelling silently in deep space.

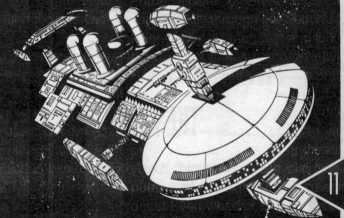

11

It is programmed to return safely to Earth in 500 years.

Everything on board is working perfectly. There's just one problem ...

... all the crew are dead.

What happened on board *Warp 9* had nothing to do with humans, or aliens, or any living creatures.

It was something that the crew could never have predicted ...

Thinking Machines
THE FACTS

You're an astronaut. Your name is Dave. You're one of a crew in a spaceship that's set to explore the outer reaches of the solar system.

Although your mission is important, you don't have a lot to do just now. The ship is flown, maintained and controlled by the world's most advanced computer. Voice recognition and speech are both built in, which means you can talk direct to the computer, and it can answer back. It even has a name. That name is HAL.

HAL is soft-spoken, helpful and polite. When you first switched him on, he announced, 'I am fully operational and all my circuits are functioning perfectly.' It was a very reassuring message.

But now something has gone wrong. The

fellow members of your crew are being killed off one by one. And you've just discovered the cause. Every one of them died while using the computer.

You don't understand why this is happening, except that clearly it's some sort of malfunction. Maybe there's a bug in the program. Maybe cosmic radiation has affected the silicon chips. But there's an obvious solution. The computer has to be shut down. It's a serious step, but you're prepared to take it. After all, you're a qualified pilot. You may not be able to fly the ship as expertly as HAL, but you can certainly get it home if all else fails. So you sit down at the console, access voice control and instruct the computer to shut down, pending repairs.

And in that quiet voice of his, HAL replies, 'I'm sorry, Dave. I can't do that.'

This chilling story was part of the action in Arthur C. Clarke's most popular novel, *2001, A Space Odyssey*, which became an equally popular movie under the expert direction of Stanley Kubrick. Both book and movie told the same story. The computer took complete control of the spaceship despite the efforts of the human crew. What made the whole thing so frightening was the suggestion that computers could turn on their makers.

Although Clarke denied it, many of his fans believed that HAL was meant to be one step ahead of IBM, since the letters of his name are very like a code. H comes immediately before I in the alphabet; A comes before B; L comes before M. But whether Clarke meant it or not, is it possible that computers may one day take over and begin to run the humans who created them?

Monster Machine

In 1946 the world had only one computer, an astonishing contraption known as ENIAC. The initials stand for Electronic Numerical Integrator And Computer, and the brute was housed in the University of Pennsylvania in the USA. It contained 18,000 vacuum tubes (or valves) that heated up in no time, and it whizzed along at breakneck speed, performing several hundred multiplications per minute. If you use an up-to-date computer at home or at school, the chances are that it can carry out at least a million calculations every *second* and today's really fast supercomputers whizz along at several thousand times the speed of ENIAC/your PC. But the great slow beast that was ENIAC had its program hard-wired into the processor. If you wanted to modify it, you got out your screwdriver.

The smallest piece of information a computer can handle is called a 'bit' (short for '*bi*nary dig*it*'). All a bit tells you is whether something is switched on or switched off, whether a particular value is set to 1 or 0.

Eight bits make up a 'byte', which is a lot more useful than a bit. One of the things you can do with a byte is define a letter of the alphabet, and this is why bytes are sometimes referred to as 'characters'. Early computers had a capacity measured in 'kilobytes', each of which equals 1,024 bytes. With a one-kilobyte capacity, your computer could write a short piece of text 1,000 characters long – that's about 200 words. It isn't a lot, but the first personal computers made do with 28-kilobyte capacities.

In the days of ENIAC, a soothsayer (who must have been a descendant of the character who predicted that London would soon be buried in horse manure) confidently announced that a one-megabyte computer (one that would hold 1,048,576 bytes of information) was impossible. He'd worked out that you'd need a structure bigger than the Empire State Building to house it in and a water source the equivalent of Niagara Falls to cool down all those vacuum tubes.

In 1974, however, Micro Instrumentation Telemetry Systems (MITS) started to sell a computer kit called Altair by mail order in the USA. Altair didn't have a single vacuum tube and it was so much smaller than the Empire State Building that it could sit on top of the average desk. The demand for the Altair was incredible. In 1977 Tandy Corporation (known in the USA as Radio Shack) jumped on the bandwagon with a personal computer that was already assembled. It had a keyboard and a monitor, and you could program it yourself and store the information on cassette tape. Also in 1977, a young American named Steve Wozniak put down his soldering iron in his garage, having just put together Apple I, the first personal computer with a disk drive. A revolution was under way.

Today, multi-megabyte computers are commonplace, but it's not at all clear whether this gives them the muscle to take us over. The whole question of such a takeover is linked to the fascinating subject of artificial intelligence.

What's Intelligence?

A lot of people think that intelligence is about being clever or knowing things, but it isn't actually as simple as that. Intelligence is the *ability* to learn or to understand, not the amount of information that's been stuffed into your brain. Intelligence is what allows you to deal with new situations, and it can also be seen in the way you use the knowledge you've already gained.

For a long time now, experts have looked for ways of measuring intelligence, using everything from IQ (Intelligence Quotient) tests to end-of-term exams. But the honest ones among them will admit that none of the tests is perfect. Take the case of Winston Churchill, for example. Your history books will tell you that he became Prime Minister of Great Britain, led his country successfully through the Second World War, was knighted by his monarch and is known as one of the greatest statesmen of the twentieth century. He also managed to fail the entrance exam for Harrow School when he was a boy.

Artificial intelligence (often called AI) is even trickier to grasp. It's simple to write a computer program that answers 'I understand' every time you make an input. But claiming that the computer understands doesn't mean that it really does. Even when computers were programmed to play games that test your brainpower – like chess – the difficulties surrounding AI refused to go away. Although a chess program might be good enough to beat you hollow, this still doesn't mean that it's intelligent.

Man v. Machine

The way computers began to play chess was quite different from the way a human being plays. Basically, a computer would blindly 'try out' different moves until its time ran out, then it would play the one that left it in the best position. With a fast computer and a good program, the try-out process could run to hundreds or even thousands of moves.

How do humans play a game like chess that needs thought? In so far as we can understand it at all, (human) Chess Grandmasters work like this:

1 Like the computer, players try out various moves in their imagination before making the real one. The number of try-outs will not be anything like as many as the computer makes – but, unlike a computer, humans will know, from instinct or experience, that certain moves are not worth trying, they're just plain silly.

2 Humans will search for patterns – moves they've made before when the pieces were in much the same positions as they're in now. Once they find a pattern, they know that making the same move as they made last time is likely to lead to the same result.

3 As humans, they are flexible enough to react to their opponent's play rather than simply following a blind try-out procedure. They're able to read and take advantage of their opponent's psychology and habits of play.

4 Finally, they will often use intuition to decide on the best move.

This is entirely different from the way early computers played. They couldn't learn from experience and they couldn't react to an opponent's style of play. Because of this, experts confidently predicted that, while computers might beat the duffers of the chess world, they would never defeat a grandmaster.

Computer Chess Champ

Then, in 1997, an IBM computer program called Deeper Blue was matched against Chess Grandmaster Gary Kasparov.

Kasparov was the world champion, and he had pitted himself against computers before. Until now he had won every time. Just a year before, he had trounced Deep Blue, the best program IBM could come up with at the time. Kasparov was confident he could do the same again with Deeper Blue.

The first game went to Kasparov. But in the second, Deeper Blue, which had been designed to consider up to *four million* positions before making a move, became the first computer in history to beat a Grandmaster. The crowd rewarded its victory with a resounding cheer.

Did this astonishing result mean that Deeper Blue was more intelligent than Kasparov? Not really. It may have beaten him at chess, but it couldn't write a letter in

Kasparov tries to work out a way of outwitting the computer, Deeper Blue.

20

Russian, drive a car or order burger and chips – all things Kasparov could do easily. Outside of chess, Deeper Blue was a complete idiot.

So deciding when a computer is intelligent isn't as easy as it seems. In fact, once you start to think about it, it's very difficult to figure out what really adds up to artificial intelligence.

One of the earliest computer engineers, the Englishman Alan Turing, wrestled with the problem. There was no doubt at all about Turing's own intelligence – he was an expert code-breaker during the Second World War. After considerable thought, he came up with a test to tell whether a machine was intelligent.

Turing Test

His idea was that you first set up two terminals, one connected to a human being, the other to a computer. Next, you allow people to ask any question they like at either terminal. If they can't tell when they're talking to the human being, then the computer is displaying intelligence.

Since the Turing Test was first devised, an endless stream of software designers have tried to beat it. One who came close was a computer scientist called Joseph Weizenbaum.

Back in 1966, Dr Weizenbaum was teaching at the Massachusetts Institute of Technology. In his spare time he created a program he called ELIZA, after Eliza Doolittle, the character in

George Bernard Shaw's play, *Pygmalion*.

In the play, Eliza Doolittle started out as an ignorant working girl, but eventually she learned enough to pass herself off as a lady. Dr Weisenbaum's computer program did much the same thing. As you used it, it learned more and more about you until it was able to pass itself off as an intelligent being.

ELIZA was made up of two parts; one was the program's main routine and the other was what Weisenbaum called a 'script'. With different scripts, ELIZA could carry on sensible conversations on various topics.

This was how it worked. You sat down at the keyboard and typed in something to start the conversation. The main routine of the program would take what you'd typed and use it to produce a sensible answer. Then you'd type something in return, and the whole thing would be repeated and, before you knew it, you were having what felt like an intelligent conversation.

Computer Chat

One of the scripts Weizenbaum prepared for ELIZA allowed the program to pretend it was a psychiatrist. You told it your problems and it helped you tease out some answers. Here's an example of the way ELIZA responded, based on my own input:

Hello.
HELLO. MY NAME IS ELIZA. WHAT'S YOURS?
Herbie.
WHAT WOULD YOU LIKE TO TALK ABOUT TODAY, HERBIE?
I have a problem.
HOW DO YOU FEEL ABOUT HAVING A PROBLEM?
I feel I want to talk to you about it.
AND IF YOU GOT TO TALK TO ME ABOUT IT, WOULD THAT HELP?
Yes, I think so.
WHAT MAKES YOU BELIEVE SO? PLEASE BE SPECIFIC.
You're some sort of psychiatrist, aren't you?
I DEFINITELY AM NOT.
Let me tell you my problem anyway.
I AM LISTENING. TELL ME MORE.
I have fallen in love with a Spice Girl.
ARE YOU AN AFFECTIONATE PERSON?
Generally yes.
WHY 'GENERALLY YES'?
Oh, all right, I am an affectionate person.
SO YOU ARE AN AFFECTIONATE PERSON. DO YOU ENJOY IT?
Of course I do.
YOU SEEM TO HAVE GIVEN THAT ASSERTION

```
A LOT OF THOUGHT.
Can we stop here?
IF YOU WERE ME, WOULD YOU STOP HERE?
Yes.
ARE YOU REALLY POSITIVE?
Yes.
IT HELPS TO KEEP A POSITIVE ATTITUDE.
```

In point of fact, the whole idea worked *too* well. When students at the Institute discovered the program on its computer network, they spent so much time discussing their love lives with ELIZA that the entire system ground to a halt!

It is perfectly possible that with a little more refinement, a larger database and a faster response-time – all possible with modern computers – ELIZA could be made to pass the Turing Test. But would that mean the program was intelligent? Clearly not. As we have seen, the program only *appeared* to be intelligent. What it actually did was to take bits from what you typed in and feed them back to you in accordance with a specific set of rules.

This points to a problem with the test itself. ELIZA was software designed, not to simulate intelligence, but rather to mimic personality. That's what makes you think you're talking to another human being. Cast your mind back over the last few conversations you've had, the ones about football or the way you style your hair. If you're honest, you'll have to admit intelligence had very little to do with them.

But, Turing Test or not, computer engineers are still hard at work trying to create a machine that will exhibit genuine reasoning power. To this end there have been two interesting developments. One is software that learns by experience.

Learning the Hard Way

This is an obvious approach, once you start to think about it. Learning by experience is certainly what you and I do. Remember when you were a little kid and your mother kept telling you not to get too close to the fire? Did you listen? Of course not. But the day you finally stuck your hand in the fire, you *learned by experience*. It hurt so much you decided never to do that again. It's a survival thing that stops us doing the same stupid things over and over again. And you might say that the fewer stupid things you do, the smarter you get.

It was learning by experience that allowed Deep Blue to defeat Grandmaster Kasparov eventually. In match after match, the program learned by its mistakes and the code literally rewrote itself to ensure that it would not make the same mistakes again. Deep Blue became Deeper Blue, and Deeper Blue was good enough to win.

There is no theoretical limit to the learning process, so software can go on indefinitely, getting better and better at what it does. If what it does is play chess, nobody worries except Grandmasters. But the same learn-by-experience routines are being used in more general programs, letting them get smarter and smarter.

Once the software designers develop a genuine artificial intelligence program, these routines will make sure that it quickly becomes *more intelligent* than its creators. In a few (software) generations, it could become more intelligent than anyone on the planet.

As usual, science fiction has tested just this outcome. The movie *The Matrix* was all about machines that got so smart they finally went to war with humans ... and won. And one of the most disturbing stories ever written describes how all the computers on the planet are finally linked to make one huge super-computer that knows absolutely everything. At the official opening ceremony, the World President puts the question that everybody wants answered: 'Is there a God?'

And the supercomputer replies, 'There is now.'

The second development is, if anything, even more disturbing. This is the use of computers to design and build more advanced computers. Here again, the controlling software contains learning and feedback routines that make sure each new generation of hardware is more sophisticated and efficient than the last. The process has *already* created experimental computers which work in ways the (human) project engineers no longer fully understand. Fortunately, the improvements have been confined to the efficiency of the hardware . . . at least for now.

Put together these two developments, and it is clear that real machine intelligence is on its way. If this is so, it is difficult to see why intelligent machines would be prepared to keep taking orders from stupid humans. It's beginning to look as if HAL really could take over . . . and very, very soon.

But we've got something coming up to take your mind off that little worry. Turn the page for the first of our special sections on past technology predictions that went right . . . and some that went very wrong.

Yes ... No ... Maybe?

The first of three special sections on predictions made ten years ago about technology in the New Millennium

Do you ever watch the TV re-runs of the old sci-fi *Flash Gordon* movies that were made in the 1930s as serials for the Saturday-morning picture shows? The really old ones, where the spaceships buzzed like lawnmowers and the Third Millennium technology all looked like wireless sets from the 1950s? It's always fun to see what people predicted years ago as the technology of tomorrow, and then compare it with the reality of today.

In these sections you get to hear about some things that were forecast and then you find out whether the jury verdict on each guess is 'Yes, they got it right', 'No, that was way off-key', or 'Maybe', which means we can't be sure yet.

....

Prediction: Computerized interior design
Result: The prediction was that computers would take the guesswork out of designing a home by creating 3-D models on-screen to

your specification. They did and they do. You can now get a program that allows you to try out different paint colours on your walls, move your furniture around and rebuild bits of your house . . . all without having to move away from your PC. This one is a definite 'Yes'.

Prediction: Voice keys

Result: Voice-recognition technology developed years ago by a US company meant that you could set up a security system at home which responded to your voice and yours alone, a bit like Ali Baba and his 'Open Sesame'. Great if you keep losing your key or forgetting what numbers you should tap into those combination locks. Surprisingly, there's still no sign of it catching on, though. Probably a 'No', unless they bring the price down.

Prediction: Portable voice-activated translators

Result: Six years and several million dollars went into the development of *Voice*, a more or less portable (it weighed nearly 3lb – that's over a kilogram) translating device, more than a decade ago. You talk into it in English, and it translates your words directly into German or whatever. Another neat idea, coming close to *Star Trek*'s universal translator, and one that could make real inroads yet. Your local gizmo shop will sell you any number of electronic translators, some little bigger than a credit card. You won't find many that are voice-activated though. This one is a 'Maybe'.

. . . .

Prediction: Self-weeding lawns
Result: These were predicted, following the discovery by a Canadian scientist of a grass that poisons, strangles, uproots or otherwise somehow kills off nearby weeds. You'd imagine it would have taken over the world by now, but it hasn't. Self-weeding lawns remain a pipe-dream. A definite 'No'.

. . . .

Prediction: CD-ROMs
Result: Hard to believe it now, but back in 1990 writers on computers had to explain that a CD-ROM was a silver disk that could *actually hold the entire, 12-volume Oxford English Dictionary*! Wow! If anybody had mentioned *Doom* or *Quake*, they might have been too scared to invent these amazing silver disks. But they didn't, and they did. A 'Yes', as you already know.

. . . .

Prediction: Weather cubes
Result: Toshiba invented the ten-centimetre

(four-inch) battery-powered cube that predicted the weather eight hours in advance by displaying the appropriate symbol on an LCD
screen. You'd imagine everybody in England
would have one by now, given the national
obsession with the weather, but Michael Fish
still has his job. Sorry, Toshiba, it's a 'No'.

....

Prediction: Video telephones
Result: This prediction has been on the cards
for ever and was probably being chipped on to
rock by science-fiction writers in the Stone
Age. A working videophone was actually
shown at the New York World Fair in 1964, with
threats of widespread introduction just about
every year since then. It's one of those all-time
great inventions that nobody actually wants,
probably because it won't let you pretend you
have the 'flu; but there does seem to be a
move towards widespread video-conferencing
via the Internet, which is sort of similar. Call it a
'Maybe'.

....

Prediction: Larger-than-life TV
Result: Current TV technology means that
there's a limit to how far your picture size can
go before your set gets bigger than your living
room. Alternative technologies like TV projec-
tion systems have traditionally suffered from

quality problems, but I saw a beauty in the United States just last year in which the people on the screen were almost life size. The technology is definitely coming, along with flat screens you can roll up and put away in a drawer when they aren't hanging on the wall. Wait for it – this one's a 'Yes'.

Prediction: Motion simulator movies
Result: Back in 1990 some idiot predicted that people in the year 2000 would actually pay good money to visit movie houses in which hydraulically operated seats would throw them back and forth in time to roller-coaster action movies (sick bags provided). The good (?) news is: the first such theatres have already opened in the USA. Practise your projectile vomiting and give that one an unexpected 'Yes'.

Prediction: Electronic still photography
Result: What that means is 'digital cameras'. Digital cameras take their pictures electronically and store them in the same way as your PC does, so you can load them into a computer, view them on screen and draw a moustache on your aunt, using your favourite paint program. The prediction has come true, and soon the price should have come down far enough for you to be able to afford one. Another 'Yes'.

The Robots Are Coming!
THE FACTS

Strictly speaking, a robot is any automatically operated machine that does the work a human used to do. The very name comes from the Czech word *robota*, which means 'forced labour'. A robot doesn't have to have arms and legs. It doesn't have to look like a human at all.

But that's not usually the way the science-fiction writers see it.

It was clear to early science-fiction writers that robots, when we got around to inventing them, would have to look like people. It was the only logical design. They argued that we'd already invested vast sums of money in developing technology like tractors, motor cars, lawnmowers, aeroplanes and computer key-boards. All these things had been designed for human beings – you needed human hands and feet to operate them.

So which would be the best way to go? Do you invent a robot tractor, then start all over again and invent a robot car, then a robot lawn-mower, then a robot aeroplane? Of course you don't. The cost would be ridiculous. It would make far more sense to manufacture robots that looked like human beings. They could then be programmed to drive the tractor, fly the aeroplane or type at the computer keyboard.

As sensible people, sci-fi writers decided that the robots were coming . . . and they had to look like humans. And not just a little like humans. R2D2 might be cute, but he was far from typical. Almost every famous sci-fi robot has had two arms, two legs, a body and a head. Some of them, like Data in *Star Trek: The Next Generation*, looked so much like humans you could hardly tell them apart. (Don't let's get into a discussion about the fact that under the face-paint Data is in reality just an actor pre-tending to be a robot, and that an actor is much cheaper to employ than a robot-like machine is to build and control.)

Data-type robots are technically known as androids, machines made to mimic humans in every respect. (Just to confuse things further, cyborgs are a combination of machine parts

The android, Data, blends in nicely with the humans in Star Trek: First Contact.

and living tissue.) It was androids that Isaac Asimov was really writing about in his famous *I, Robot* series.

Asimov's robots had names like R. Daneel. The 'R' stood for 'Robot' and was designed to alert people that they weren't dealing with another human being. This was important in the future Asimov created, because people didn't like robots one little bit. It's difficult to know why, because robots were all made in accordance with Asimov's three very special laws.

Laws of Robotics

1 No robot shall harm a human being.

2 No robot shall by inaction allow a human being to come to harm, provided this does not conflict with the First Law.

3 A robot shall seek to preserve its own existence, provided this does not conflict with the First or Second Laws.

Although Dr Asimov was a scientist as well as a sci-fi writer, the laws were pure fiction. But despite this, they are still to this day considered to be the best possible basis for robot design. Not that robot design has got very far.

Everyday Robots

Contrary to all the science-fiction predictions, we in the real world have concentrated on making individual machines more smart. Thus an autopilot is now built into every commercial aeroplane so the captain can drink tea and chat while the plane flies itself. Cars have computers built in to tell you when anything goes wrong and to control the suspension or the amount of fuel you use. Some cars have computers that will guide you all the way to your destination even if you haven't a clue how to get there. The sort of intelligent sports car once driven only by David Hasselhoff in the TV science-fiction series, *Knightrider*, is just around the corner. You may even be able to buy it by the time you read this.

But if we haven't exactly followed what the sci-fi writers predicted, we have made a little progress on the robot front. In the car industry, for example, computer-controlled robot devices have, since 1960, more or less taken the place of people on the assembly lines. These robots mimic the movements of human arms and hands so that they can lift, weld and spray-paint car bodies. Some high-performance robots have built-in sensors to keep them on the right track. Others are equipped with cameras which continually scan their work and compare it with built-in designs.

You'll find robots of this type in almost every other industry that uses an assembly line. There are single-arm robots drilling and riveting body sections of aircraft. Electronics companies use robots to sort and test finished products.

Despite these developments, however, a society in which humans live and work with androids like Data seems as far away as ever. In the late 1970s, a wealthy magazine proprietor unveiled a mechanical servant that could look after his guests at cocktail parties. This little fellow looked vaguely human in shape and wheeled around the room with a drinks tray. Built-in sensors meant it didn't collide with anything and knew (most of the time) when it had reached a human being. It would then activate a recording that invited you to name your poison and it held up the tray for you to select your drink. It was certainly a fun machine but, while it was promoted as the world's first real-life robot, its abilities were so limited it seemed to be just one step away from a toy.

Nobody rushed to improve it. A scientist in Edinburgh created a prototype robot arm that could play chess, but failed to provide the rest of the body. A build-your-own robot kit, selling for around £300, allowed you to bolt together a smallish creature that could be programmed to carry out simple tasks like detecting burglars with its infra-red sensors and then frightening them away with cries of 'Help! Police!'

When the kit was finally withdrawn, this brief attempt to sell robots like dishwashers or TV sets died a welcome death. The term 'robot' – which dates back to a play by Karel Capek called *R. U. R.* ('Rossum's Universal Robots'), first presented in 1921 – is still used mainly to describe automated production processes in the automobile and other industries. When my editor was offered a beer by a robot waiter in a Japanese restaurant the other day, the creature turned out to be no more than a talking trolley that stopped if you clapped your hands.

Although there's now a popular TV programme called *Robot Wars* in which machines compete with one another like gladiators in Ancient Rome, these aren't real robots either. They're actually just remote-controlled devices with a few built-in fighting functions.

So, will Rossum never build a universal robot? Is Data fated to remain a figment of the script-writer's imagination? Will we only ever see a robot when the Daleks finally invade?

Walkies, K9!

There are several problems that remain to be solved before we can build a humanoid robot, most of them unexpected. One of the most difficult is teaching it to walk on two legs.

Walking on two legs comes so naturally to us that we never stop to think how we do it. In fact if we *do* stop to think, we quickly realize that we don't actually know. We learned the trick by trial and error when we were little, then thankfully turned the whole process over to another type of robot – the one that lives deep in our subconscious mind. Now, we just walk. We don't think about it, we get on with it.

But in fact the whole process of walking upright involves a complicated sequence of muscle movements, feedback and adjustments. Even standing upright is an ongoing series of checks, balances and corrections.

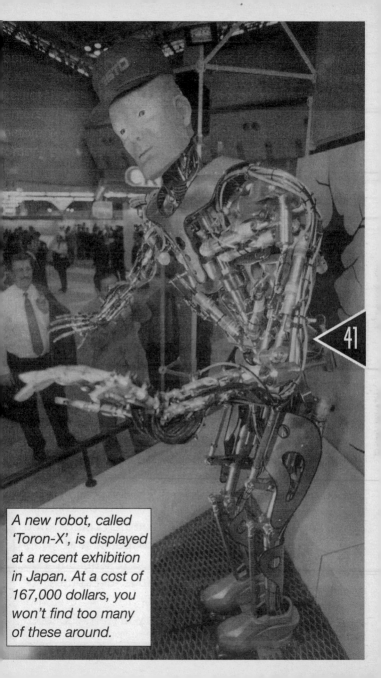

41

A new robot, called 'Toron-X', is displayed at a recent exhibition in Japan. At a cost of 167,000 dollars, you won't find too many of these around.

There are literally thousands – sometimes millions – of calculations needed to allow you to do the simplest thing.

This number of calculations is no longer beyond modern computers, but it is beyond any modern computer *we can fit into the same space as the human brain*. And that's just walking. A humanoid robot has to be able to avoid obstacles, talk, interact and, if it's going to be useful, carry out at least a few simple tasks like making your meals, picking up after you and tidying your room.

But before a mechanical servant can do any of that, it needs to recognize who you are – and that, too, has proved an unexpectedly difficult problem in robot research.

Seeing Things

What scientists call 'pattern recognition' (which includes the ability to recognize friends from their appearance or even their walk) comes easy to human beings, and we do it very well – too well, in fact, which is why it's so easy for us to see faces in clouds and pictures in the fire. But the ability isn't hard-wired in the brain. It's a learned response and, while most other animals also learn it quickly and easily, it presents enormous difficulties for machines.

The trouble may be that you learn it at such

an early age, long before you started to walk or talk. It began, so far as scientists have been able to determine, before you could even focus your eyes properly. The whole thing seems to be based on an even more primitive mechanism called 'imprinting'.

Mummy! Mummy!

Some of the best – and definitely the most amusing – research into imprinting was carried out by the naturalist, Konrad Lorenz, who made a study of young ducks.

In the wild, it is important that you recognize your mother. If you don't stick with her when you're little, your chances of being eaten increase considerably. Lorenz discovered that evolution has developed an instinctive process in ducklings – and in many other birds and animals – to solve this problem.

What happens is that a chick emerging from the egg will automatically imprint on the first big moving thing it sees. Since nine times out of ten the first big moving thing it sees will be the mother duck, this works rather well. The little duckling tucks safely in behind her, imitates her walk, and the whole new family waddles off to find the nearest pond.

But when Lorenz was carrying out his studies – which, like any good naturalist, meant he had to get up close and personal – the first big moving thing a lot of ducklings saw was Lorenz himself. As a result, he soon found himself being trailed by a string of adoring ducklings, each one convinced he was its mother.

Fortunately, human babies don't fix on things in quite this way. But they do develop a remarkable ability to recognize their parents from a very early age. For a human, the basic pattern of the mother's face – two eyes, a nose and (hopefully) a smiling mouth – seems to be understood instinctively from the moment it is born. On this early foundation, all the rest of our excellent pattern recognition skills are built.

As with walking, you get so good at pattern recognition that you quickly forget how difficult it really is. But you can remind yourself with a simple experiment. All you have to do is write down a description of your best friend's face so that a total stranger would be *absolutely certain* to recognize him or her in a crowd of 20,000. Tricky, eh? That's how difficult it is to write a recognition program for a robot.

Currently, pattern recognition forms a major part of robotics research and, while it's a slow, uphill struggle, things are improving. Robot eyes and robot brains can now do rather better than telling the difference between a cube and a pyramid. But they still would have a lot of trouble recognizing your friend in a crowd of 20,000 – something you can do in the blink of an eye.

Tomorrow's Robots

One solution to the walking and the pattern recognition problems is sheer raw computing power, something that has been increasing dramatically for years. The same mindset that buried London under horse manure and predicted powerful computers would need Niagara to cool their valves now confidently says we will never build a computer to match the human brain. Isaac Asimov solved this problem in his fictional robots by inventing something called a 'positronic brain', only he forgot to mention how to make it. And without that sort of invention, androids like Data must remain a fiction.

Admittedly the human brain is a remarkable achievement. You have more cells in your brain than there are stars in the sky. Some experts believe that your creative capacity is boundless. Certainly you seem able to store every experience and impression you have ever had, every sight and sound you have ever seen and heard. (You don't normally remember them, but they can be brought to the surface by exciting certain areas of the brain with an electrode.)

Your brain is also exceptionally well packaged. It takes up less than 1,350 cubic centimetres (83 cubic inches) inside your skull.

Matching it with a portable computer that can process and store a lifetime of data is well beyond today's technology. But scientists are working on advanced computers that promise vast storage and computing power in ever smaller packages. And this means that the day may be close at hand when a skull-sized positronic brain like Data's will become a working reality.

Meanwhile you may be interested to learn that a smart vacuum-cleaner has just come on the market. It can't climb stairs, but it will zip around cleaning the downstairs of your home without knocking over that can of Coke you keep leaving on the floor . . .

Chapter 4

Lost in Cyberspace

Jennifer has undergone an operation to get 'wireheaded' – having a computer chip planted in her brain. She's just waking up ...

On returning home she can't wait to plug herself into her computer ...

47

... where she'll be transported to a different world ...

It's a place where she can be anyone, do anything – who needs reality?

Lost in Cyberspace

THE FACTS

Nobody predicted cyberspace. There have been lots of sci-fi stories about what might happen to it, how it might affect your life, where it might be going. But these have all been written *after* cyberspace came into being. Nobody saw it coming in advance, probably because nobody really foresaw the Internet that gave it birth. Not even the people who *invented* the Internet foresaw the Internet.

Everybody thinks the Internet started in the United States. Actually, it didn't. The *idea* of the Net certainly arose in America, but it was the National Physical Laboratory in Britain that put together the first few computer links in 1968. They were based on plans designed to create a system that would still function after you dropped a bomb on it.

When the NPL proved that the ideas worked, the American military – who had commissioned the study that produced the ideas in the first place – decided to try them out for real . . . which they did in 1969 by linking together four supercomputers.

Hard though it is to believe, those four super-computers, each one probably less powerful than the PC on your desk, were the start of the Internet. And the Internet was the start of cyber-space.

Today uncounted millions of people are linked into the Internet. With an estimated 10 million joining every *month*, it's impossible to quote an accurate figure. And if the Net itself is composed of untold millions of interlinked com-puters, cyberspace is the picture you have in your head of the stuff that's in those links. This is a difficult idea to grasp at first, but you can see what it's all about very quickly once you look at the Internet in action.

Cybercity Life

Fortune City is Europe's fastest-growing urban sprawl. (You can visit it yourself on the World Wide Web at http://www.fortunecity.com.) It has streets and houses, shopping malls and sports grounds. It has its own social clubs where peo-ple get together and its own casino where they

**This district is
for people
fascinated
by the occult
and unexplained.**

CLICK HERE TO GET 20Mb FREE WEB SPACE

HOME | DISTRICTS | BUILDING SITE | SHOPPING | FUNSTUFF | HELP

Check out this week's recommended sites
- Star Trek Voyager - A complete information guide
- A.R.K. - Get close to heaven with the Holy Scripture
- Buffy's Vampire Demons - The vampire tales
- The Opal Path - Read the paranance ability
- Neon Genesis Evangelion - Stories to experience
- The Star Wars Archive - The best information source
- Roswell District Headquarters - Health information
- Croswell - Meet our Roswell Minister
- Roswell Minister in Centre
- Cera Ann - Meet our fantastic Floating Minister

50

*If you're a bit of a spooky
soul, why not take up
residence in Fortune City
Paranormal District?*

can gamble money. It has a pirate radio station
and a lottery. It elects its own mayor. It has its
own laws and law enforcement. It has its own
building sites. When you become a citizen, you
select a property in the sort of district that
interests you, the authorities put up a notice-
board to say that the site is taken and they help
you move your stuff in when you're ready.

At least that's what Fortune City is in cyberspace. In physical reality, it's a collection of
files on a large computer. There are scores of
sites like that. Fortune City is just one Net
metropolis among many. Beyond it there are
rooms – and at least one palace – where peo-

ple gather to chat. There are libraries packed with books. There are racetracks. There are universities. There are complete *worlds* (called Multi-User Dungeons) where you can fight monsters and discover magic. In every case, in physical reality these wonders are no more than information traces on magnetic disks.

Thus cyberspace is something absolutely unique in human history. It is imagination driven by the information flow of a computer network. It is the dreams of millions of people, built on bits and bytes. No wonder nobody predicted it. It is just too weird for words.

But if nobody saw it coming, there are science-fiction books (like *Rim* or William Gibson's *Neuromancer*) that are all too anxious to tell us where it's going. Most of them take it for granted that cyberspace is somehow going to get more 'real'. A sub-plot of *Rim* describes how a computer crash causes an enormous Japanese cybercity to disappear . . . along with all its human citizens. Is this possible? Not the disappearing citizens, of course, but the idea that cyberspace may eventually develop from a collective, computer-driven daydream into something far more tangible? The answer to that lies in the heady realm of virtual reality.

Get Virtual

At its most basic, a virtual reality interface for

your computer consists of a special helmet incorporating earphones and goggles with, maybe, some sort of joystick or handset attached. It lets you play fairly simple games – the sort of shoot-'em-ups you've probably enjoyed on your monitor screen. The gimmick with virtual reality is that it makes you feel you're actually *inside* the game. The earphones provide surround sound. The goggles mean that, as you turn your head, the scene you're watching scrolls in time with your movement.

Not such a long time ago, even that simple set-up would have cost you more than £30,000. At the time of writing, it's about as expensive as a home video-recorder. By the time you read this, the price will probably have dropped again. Even so, nobody's getting too excited about virtual reality yet. The graphic quality is still poor, the animation still clunky. It doesn't look real and it doesn't feel real.

But, as computing power continues to increase, what's promised for the world of tomorrow is nothing short of mind-blowing. Already available (if you've a rig that will support it and a friend in the research lab) is the virtual reality glove. You wear this in addition to the helmet. It has built-in pressure-pads and sensors so that, when you meet a computer character in a virtual reality adventure and it takes your hand, you can actually *feel* the handshake. The glove also lets you fondle one or two simple objects.

Also available, at least in the experimental workshops, is the virtual reality treadmill. You stand on this, wearing your helmet and glove, and you can actually physically 'walk' around in a computer-generated environment.

If all this is beginning to sound a little spooky, you ain't heard nothing yet! In Japan, they're currently working to develop 'smart skin'. Smart skin is a sort of body stocking that doesn't come with sensors like the glove, but is *itself* a sensor. When perfected, smart skin will allow you to experience computer-generated sensations anywhere on your body, including blows delivered in a virtual fight. If it works as well as everyone is hoping it will, safeguards will have to be built in – otherwise a virtual opponent could knock you out or even kill you.

But even smart skin has its limitations. It won't allow you to taste or smell things, for example. The leading-edge technology most experts are now backing is something far more weird.

Wireheading

Wireheading comes straight out of a Frankenstein movie. If it happens, it will involve having your brain opened up by a surgeon and a computer chip put inside. This chip is then wired directly (and permanently) into areas of your brain that interpret sensory input – what you see, hear, taste, touch and smell. When the surgeon is finished with you, you will have a little socket built in at the back of your head. This socket will allow you to plug your PC directly into your brain. Or, rather, it will allow you to plug your brain directly into your PC.

What all this comes down to is that the chip inside your skull will allow you to experience *absolute* virtual reality – just like Keanu Reeves in the movie *The Matrix*. In this story, all humankind are controlled by super-nasty intelligent machines that have created a virtual world for us to live in. And it is such a convincing world that nobody catches on to the fact that it isn't real (except for Keanu, of course). As the movie illustrates, once the computer cranks up a picture or a scene or an adventure game, you will be able to see it, feel it, hear it, touch it, taste it. There are no problems about graphic quality because no graphics are involved. The input stimulates your brain to create an environment *you simply can't tell from reality*. But this would be better than physical reality.

You would no longer be stuck with the body you have, for example. You could be taller, shorter, stronger, more athletic, thinner, fatter – whatever you want to be. Tired of being a redhead? You could change colour instantly, have any style you wanted . . . including a head of snakes like the Medusa. You wouldn't even need to be human any more. You could select an animal shape like a wolf or a bear or a cat. You could become a creature of fantasy: a griffin, perhaps, or a fire-breathing dragon. And if that's not eccentric enough, how about turning yourself into a fire-engine, a can of cola or a plate of chips? Remember, anything is possible and the experience *feels* absolutely real.

Your range of possibilities is generated by the computer – which is a limitation of sorts – but you can be sure that, once virtual reality takes hold, there will soon be more software choices than you could possibly experience in a lifetime.

Living Nightmare

In the early days you might have problems. There are very few computer programs that are completely bug-free, especially in their early versions. At the moment, the worst that can happen is that you crash your computer. But think how tricky it could be if you were in the middle of *living* a game. You might find yourself in a nightmare with no means of escape. If you built up enough feedback, you might even fry your brains as the chip inside your skull begins to overheat. But the programmers will sort out these little problems soon enough and, with the sort of money that's going to be earned from virtual reality, a few beta-testers might well be willing to risk their lives.

An experimental chip for wireheading has already been developed. What we're waiting for is the surgical technique to insert it safely. Even the volunteers are in place. I could give you the names of at least two professional software engineers who say they'll have the chip implanted the minute it's available . . . and they claim that most of their colleagues feel the same way.

Once the chips are in enough brains and are working well, only one last step remains in the creation of our most fascinating techno-future. That step is the use of wireheading as an Internet interface.

Net Heads

At the moment you interface with the Internet using your computer keyboard and a mouse. But already there are quite a few Internet sites which make use of a primitive form of virtual reality. They allow you to navigate (using your keyboard or mouse) through 3-D renderings of buildings or other locations. Once you plug your *head* into the Net, you will swap those crude graphics for the real thing. You will feel instantly as if you're really there.

When you visit certain Internet chat sites

today, your presence on site is marked by an 'avatar' – a little icon, possibly even a small photograph, that you can move around from place to place. This icon is identified as you and can be seen by others logged on to the site, just as you can see their icons on your screen.

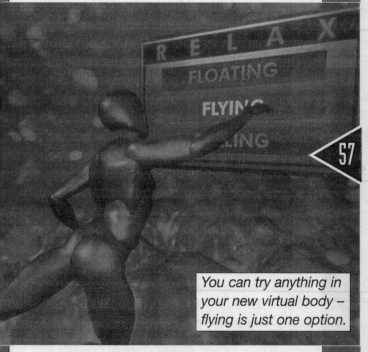

You can try anything in your new virtual body – flying is just one option.

Once you're wireheaded into the Net, those little icons are replaced by your virtual body (with which you can see, hear, taste, touch and smell, just like your real one). And, as we've already noted, your virtual body can look like

Brad Pitt or Baby Spice or anything else you feel like.

In a wireheaded virtual reality game, your virtual body is experienced only by you. Wireheaded into the Net, everybody else who's logged on can see it (or hear it or touch it) as well. They do so using the virtual bodies they have created for themselves.

New Worlds

Are you beginning to get a hint as to the possibilities? Let's take the most boring of them all – your schoolwork. Wireheading would change it completely. Physics would no longer be a series of dull equations on the blackboard. You could simply plug in and shrink to sub-atomic size to see the structures for yourself. You could hitch a ride on a photon and cross the galaxy at the speed of light. You could use an electron as your skateboard.

History would be a doddle. You could fight beside Wellington, help Harold pull the arrow from his eye, assist in the building of Stonehenge or the pyramids. You could become an Aztec sacrifice (if you were really stupid) or a policy adviser to Queen Elizabeth I. There would not be a time or place on the curriculum you could not experience directly.

In your chemistry lessons you could do all the things you've always wanted to do, like creating a high explosive to blow up your school. (This is only *virtual* reality, remember, so the pieces come together again next time you run the program.)

But it's when you're wireheaded into the Internet that your education really takes off. Why put up with your present dumb old teachers when you could have the best in the world? There are no limits to the size of a virtual class on the Net . . . and no limits to the learning experience.

Want to learn about comparative religion? The Dalai Lama will guide you as you levitate to the Potala Palace in Tibet, then listen to the monks chanting in Drepung Monastery.

Want to know about the cosmos? Stephen Hawking will accompany you to the outer reaches of the universe, then back in time to experience the Big Bang.

Pete Sampras will teach you how to play a better game of tennis. Sister Wendy will explain the Old Master you're looking at in Florence. Carol Vorderman will show you how to add.

And that's just the beginning. You could visit friends and travel anywhere in the world without ever leaving your home. You could pilot a jet plane, go for a bungee-jump, enjoy white-water rafting, take a rocket trip to Alpha Centauri. You could try your hand at open-heart surgery, safe in the knowledge you will never harm a patient.

You could shoot up bad guys, rob a bank, eat a ton of chocolate without throwing up or putting on weight. You could walk (without a spacesuit) on the moon or the bottom of the ocean. You could learn how to be a playwright from Will Shakespeare. You could take your favourite movie star out on a date.

You could build your own mansion (in a minute) and stock it with the world's finest sculptures and paintings. You could run Microsoft or IBM. You could become a were-wolf or change sex. You could make a billion dollars, then bet it on a horse. You could shrink to the size of a bacterium or grow so big you stepped from star to star.

And there would be no way – no way at all – that you could distinguish these experiences from physical reality. You would have entered a world of ultimate freedom, equipped with god-like powers. You might well be tempted never to leave . . .

Reality – Who Needs It?

And here we have the downside of this techno-future. With such pleasures and adventures waiting in cyberspace, the real world seems a dull old place. How will we ever persuade anybody to put out the rubbish or clean the windows or do anything that really needs doing?

How will *you* be persuaded to live in the real world at all? Or do you forget that altogether and arrange to have your every need serviced by the computer, right down to food and drink?

E. M. Forster, the distinguished English novelist, foresaw exactly that situation in a science-fiction short story he first published nearly a century ago. Everybody in his brave new world lived underground in their own private cell. They never went out. They didn't have to. They could communicate with each other via television screens, in much the same way as we send e-mail from our computer screens today. They lived, ate and slept their lives away against a persistent background hum. It was the hum of a single, giant machine that pumped the air they breathed, created and delivered the food they ate, generated the electricity they used and serviced their every need.

Unfortunately, Forster's story was entitled 'The Machine Stops'.

Yes ... No ... Maybe?

The second of our special sections on predictions made ten years ago about technology in the New Millennium

Here we are again with more remarkable predictions about the technology you should be enjoying today . . . if the prophets got it right yesterday.

••

Prediction: Hands-free taps

Result: Howard Hughes, the multi-billionaire, grew so concerned about germs that he used to wear empty tissue boxes on his feet. Much the same sort of thinking – and, admittedly, a sensible desire to save water – led to the development of hands-free taps. These futuristic plumbing accessories come complete with infra-red sensors that deliver a stream of water when your hands approach them and switch it off again the instant you withdraw. Despite calculations that millions of gallons would be saved if the taps were installed widely, they're not found in very many places yet. But since we now have automatic hot-air hand-driers already installed in most public loos, this one warrants a 'Maybe'.

....

Prediction: Non-shatter windows
Result: In Holland, a transparent polyester fibre sheet called Profilon Plus was predicted to put paid to shattered windows. You could actually tape a stick of dynamite to the glass and the explosion wouldn't shatter it. The manufacturers thought it would be good in bad-weather areas (to protect against tornadoes) and everybody else who heard about it thought it might be the coming thing to protect politicians under threat of assassination. Still no sign of a general introduction, but if it was designed to protect presidents we probably wouldn't get to hear about it anyway. This one is probably another 'Maybe'.

....

Prediction: Luminous golf balls
Result: Since you can't keep good players off the golf course once they reach middle age, the prediction was that by the year 2000 your parents would be playing golf all night every night with the help of luminous balls. The translucent balls were made from polyurethane with a hole for a small chemical

light-stick that emitted an eerie green glow for about six hours. But if your folks claim that was what they were doing last night, they're telling fibs. Luminous golf balls never caught on. The verdict is 'No' . . . and likely to stay that way.

....

Prediction: Deodorant knickers
Result: A chemical called Intersept promised to kill the fungus and bacteria that are the main causes of body odour. What more natural than to incorporate it into underwear at the manufacturing stage? What indeed, except that people like to wash their smalls occasionally so the chemical might soon disappear. Whatever the reason, your drawers probably smell no better than they ever did. Another 'No'.

....

Prediction: Moulded clothes
Result: Back in 1990, some far-sighted joker predicted that the day would quickly come when you'd go to your tailor, get measured by a computer, tap in your chosen colour and style, then have your clothes *moulded* to fit your body contours exactly. Great idea. Hasn't happened though. This one's a 'No'.

Prediction: Car satellite navigation

Result: This was seen as a real outside chance in 1989, although the Japanese were working on it even then. The idea was that you could link your car to a satellite system and drive around, confident in the knowledge that you could never get lost. Your car sent a radio signal to the satellite, where an on-board computer figured where the signal was coming from and sent a signal back with the information. Outsider or not, it's here – and in more than one family saloon. A 'Yes'.

Prediction: Smart pill bottles

Result: Your doctor tells you to keep taking the tablets, but instead you keep forgetting. Enter the smart pill bottle with embedded microchip that *tells* you when you've missed a dose and what to do about it. Its means of communication could be an audible alarm bell or whistle, an LCD screen or even talking to you via a voice chip. The Aprex Corporation of America took a step in the right direction several years ago with a telltale bottle that reported back to the medical computer whether you'd really taken your medicine. But so far it's not been taken any further. A 'No'.

Prediction: Walking on water

Result: There are these special shoes, right? They're made from foam and fibreglass, right? They have eight special flaps underneath and each pair weighs 13 kilos (30 lb), OK? But they let you *walk on water*, man! They were made. They were patented. But if you're thinking of buying a pair, I just don't care. That one's a 'No'. No, No, No, No, No!

....

Prediction: Dial-down movies

Result: The idea (in 1990) was that you made a phone call, placed your order, and the dial-down movie store downloaded a whole heap of first-run movies into your computer – which was of course (in the year 2000) ca-pable of viewing TV pictures. Goodbye, your friendly neighbourhood video rental shop. Well, the computer screens that let you watch TV are here. And the dial-down movies are here, but they come one at a time to your regular TV set, not to your computer, from your satellite service in the form of pay-per-view movies. And the video rental stores are still in business. Vote that one a 'Sort of'.

....

Prediction: Wristwatch pager

Result: Pagers are little electronic boxes

that tell you when somebody is trying to get hold of you on the phone. They started out very popular with doctors. Then executives began to think that it might be trendy to have one too – and the techno-prophets decided the next step was bound to be a wristwatch pager that beeped, gave you a number to ring back and directed you to use the nearest pay-phone. Turned out to be a horse-manure prediction. Along came even more trendy mobile phones to prove once again that you can't predict the future by studying current trends. Now that you can buy a mobile delicately tinted to match your bloodshot eyes, who needs a wristwatch pager? Who needs any sort of pager? Verdict: 'No'.

Prediction: Robot dog

Result: Man's best friend was all set to go robotic. An American inventor called William Holden came up with a mechanical mutt which could walk about without bumping into things, could warn postmen to go away and could obey simple commands like 'Pick that up' or 'Turn around'. And the greatest plus-point of all: you didn't even need a pooper-scooper.

In Japan, a robot dog called Aibo has recently appeared in the shops. Created by the Sony Corporation, eleven-inch tall Aibo is the ultimate virtual dog for people who prefer their pets without pongs. He can be controlled by a keyboard and has sensors in his paws as well as an antenna for a tail. When he's happy, Aibo may give you a little tune. But if he gets angry he will completely ignore all your orders (not so different from the real thing then). At a price of 250,000 yen (that's about £1,283) this robomutt may prove a little more expensive than your average pet. However, this isn't the reason why you're unlikely to see Robomutt at Crufts this year. That's because too many people in Britain prefer big, friendly, noisy, licky brutes who leave their hair on the carpet and smell like wet socks all the time. So it's 'Yes' to the robot dog – but only if you're prepared to fly to Japan.

Chapter 5

Time Machines

Thousands of years into the future, scientists are close to developing a way of travelling through time.

We may become 'time tourists', people who can choose to journey to the past ...

... or into the future.

But not all scientists agree with it ...

Time Travel a disaster waiting to happen.

Time tourism means that history could be changed – and playing with time could have disastrous consequences ...

Time Machines

THE FACTS

H. G. Wells was one of the first sci-fi writers to tackle time travel. His novel, *The Time Machine*, told the story of a Victorian inventor who constructed a time machine and used it to explore the future.

Mark Twain took up the theme in *A Connecticut Yankee in King Arthur's Court,* a vastly entertaining fantasy about . . . well, about a Connecticut Yankee in King Arthur's Court. Said American gent found himself mysteriously catapulted back through time to Camelot, where his knowledge of future technology quickly gained him a reputation as a magician, to the intense irritation of the wizard Merlin.

Since then there have been numerous science-fiction forays through time. The *Magazine* of *Fantasy and Science Fiction* ran a brilliantly crafted short story called *Time Lord*, describing the impact on Nazi Germany of a visitor from the future. It was written (modest cough) by me. *Back to the Future,* starring Michael J. Fox as a time-travelling teenager, proved such a popular movie that the studios promptly made two more of them. Since then, many more movies of the same type have been produced, *Time Bandits . . . Time Cop . . . Terminator I . . . Terminator II* to name only a few.

These offerings have all been based on the idea that time travel is actually possible. But is it?

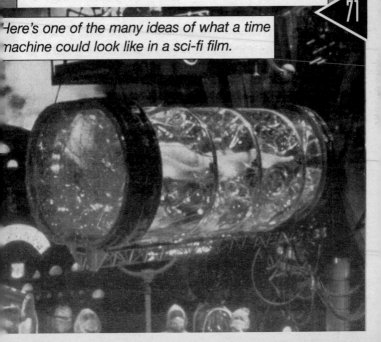

Here's one of the many ideas of what a time machine could look like in a sci-fi film.

A Closer Look at Time

Professor Albert Einstein thought it was. When he did the calculations for his famous Theories of Relativity, he discovered something very unexpected. Once you start moving, time slows down. And the faster you move, the more it slows.

You won't notice this effect on a leisurely stroll to the chip-shop. You won't even notice it in a racing car. In both cases, time actually does slow a little, but not enough to be measured. But you can measure the difference in an aeroplane, and scientists have done so by flying a super-accurate atomic clock around the world. When compared with a similar clock that stayed on the ground, there was a difference that measured a tiny fraction of a second. Time had slowed for the travelling clock.

That tiny fraction of a second shows Einstein was right, but it isn't much practical use for time travel. But when you get up near the speed of light (300,000 kilometres/186,000 miles per second), things get a lot more interesting.

Pause here for a (very) brief lesson in physics. People used to think that the smallest lump of stuff you could get was an atom. Then they cracked open atoms and found there were even smaller things inside called particles (for more information see page 123).

We now know that there is a certain type of particle called a muon, which we have managed to produce in the laboratory. Muons in the wild travel very fast at ninety-nine per cent of the speed of light. So what would happen if we found some way of travelling at muon speed?

The Space Shuttle rattles along at twenty-five times the speed of sound – about 26,550 km/h or 16,500 mph. So, outside of *Star Trek*, our fastest rockets come nowhere near the speed of light. But the problem is a purely technical one. We already know for sure what happens if you climb aboard a craft capable of muon speed. According to our calculations, time would move seven times more slowly than it does on Earth. This was worked out by Einstein in the form of his famous Twins Paradox.

The Twins Paradox

In this scenario, you have a pair of identical twins, one of whom becomes an astronaut on a spaceship capable of approaching the speed of light. The astronaut takes off to boldly go where no astronaut has gone before, while his twin stays at home to feed the cat.

Both twins are thirty years old when the astronaut leaves. The space voyage is supposed to last five years.

We're thirty.

I'm a cat.

Spaceship travels at ninety-nine per cent the speed of light

See you in five years!

He's taking a long time ...

Time moves seven times more slowly at ninety-nine per cent the speed of light

It's been five years and I'm back. But you're old!

I'm sixty-five.

... And I'm dead!

On the ship, the astronaut twin whizzes around in space for five years. So by the time he gets home again, he's thirty-five years old. But remember the muon. This spaceship is travelling at 99 per cent of the speed of light, so time is moving seven times slower on board than it is on the ground. When he arrives back on Earth, he finds that not five but thirty-five years have passed there. This means that the twin who stayed at home is now sixty-five years old and the cat is long since dead.

You now have one twin old enough to be the other's father, despite the fact that they were born at the same time. You can see why it's called a paradox: an apparent contradiction. What you may have missed is that it's also time travel. Because, when you stop thinking in terms of ageing, you realize that the astronaut twin travels thirty years into the future.

You could confirm this by comparing calendars. If the astronaut started his journey in the year 2000, the one in the ship would show the year to be 2005 when he returned. The calendars on Earth would read 2035.

That's time travel by any yardstick, and the laws of physics say it can be done. But it's a one-way trip, from the present to the future, with no means of getting back. In fact, you might think of it as time acceleration. It's a bit like the situation in prehistoric times when the first human leapt on to the back of a horse and found she could move in space far faster than she could on foot. If you leap into a near-light-speed spaceship, you can move in time far faster than you could without it.

How Far Can You Go?

But at muon speed, the furthest you could move into the future would be seven times the length of time you have left to live. If you've got ten years, you could travel only seventy years into the future before you died. If you've got twenty left, your maximum is 140 years. So you can see that, even if you started out as a baby, your maximum forward time travel at muon speed is still well under 1,000 years.

Of course you can improve this by going even faster than a wild muon – but even this has its limitations. Einstein discovered that, once you reach the full speed of light, time stops altogether and you obviously aren't going anywhere. And at any speed less than that of light, you're still going forward in time.

This is not time travel as H. G. Wells imagined it. His time machine could go back as well as forward. Is it possible that, at some time in the future, really clever scientists will invent a machine capable of taking them back in time?

On the Trail of the Time Tourists

Dr Stephen Hawking, probably the world's most famous physicist and possibly the smartest, at one time thought not. Apart from the practical problems, he wondered why we weren't swamped by time tourists travelling back from the future to see us in their past. Since clearly we aren't – how many time travellers have *you* met? – this suggests that time travel will never be developed.

But Dr Hawking's logic was wrong. It assumed that if time travel *is* developed it will be safe, easy and cheap – whereas, of course, it may be none of these things. It also assumed that the period we live in would be of interest to a future tourist. Perhaps Dr Hawking figured this out for himself, since he has recently changed his mind and announced that time travel might be possible after all.

Since we've been talking about Einstein, you may recall that he discovered that, if you ever managed to travel at 100 per cent the speed of light, time would stop. This could well lead you to wonder whether travelling faster than light would cause time to reverse and flow backwards – whether, that is, travelling faster than light would cause you to travel backwards through time.

The answer is: your suspicions are correct; travelling faster than light *would* take you back in time. But didn't Einstein also say that nothing could travel faster than light? Didn't he prove that faster-than-light travel was simply impossible?

Well . . . not quite. What he actually said was that you couldn't accelerate anything faster than the speed of light. Which may sound much the same thing, but it isn't. If you start with something that's moving at less than 300,000 kilometres a second, you can never push it beyond the speed of light. But suppose something is *already* travelling faster than the speed of light? Suppose there's something in the universe that has always naturally whizzed around at, say, 600,000 kilometres a second or more?

There's nothing in Einstein's findings to say that a natural faster-than-light object is impossible. In fact, his calculations showed that light speed would be the *lower* travel limit of such an object, not the upper.

All this may sound crazy, but physicists take it very seriously. They're currently looking for a particular type of particle called a tachyon (*tachy* means 'speedy') which naturally travels faster than the speed of light. And sure enough, the calculations show that tachyons must be moving backwards through time.

A Working Time Machine?

Tachyons are interesting, but they wouldn't be very useful even if we got our hands on some, since we don't know how to make them drive a time machine. Fortunately, however, we don't have to. A leading physicist has already published plans for a time machine which his colleagues all agree would actually work.

The physicist is Dr Frank Tipler. The plans were published in a respected scientific journal called *Physical Review*. Dr Tipler didn't call his article *How to Build a Time Machine*. He called it *Rotating Cylinders and the Possibility of*

Global Causality Violation; but how to build a time machine was exactly what it explained.

Tipler was interested in another of Einstein's discoveries: gravity warps space. We're accustomed to thinking of space as nothing, but it isn't. Space is actually something in its own right, and if you apply enough gravity to it you can twist it out of shape.

But Tipler also recalled that Einstein had discovered that space and time weren't separate. They were part of a single thing called space-time. So if gravity warped space, it had to warp time as well. Tipler reached for his calculator and worked out a really weird piece of geometry called a 'closed timelike line'.

This is going to sound silly, but a closed timelike line is the mathematical description of a path that wanders through space-time and returns to the same point it started from. But it doesn't just return to the same point in space, it comes back to the same point in time. In other words, if you find your way on to a closed timelike line, you can visit the past or the future and, however long your journey takes, you will always get back to the time when you started out.

The calculations show that there are closed timelike lines associated with Black Holes. You have to go through them twice to complete the loop. (Oddly enough, that first trip by the *Enterprise* through a Black Hole took Captain

Kirk and his crew back in time. The episode was called *Tomorrow Is Yesterday*.) Tipler started to wonder if you might be able to create closed timelike lines artificially. He concluded that if you could construct a big enough rotating cylinder, you'd create enough gravity to twist space into a closed timelike line.

But this wasn't just a case of returning to the time when you started. Because the cylinder was spinning, time would swing like a pendulum. Catch it on one swing and you'd move forward into the future. Catch it on another and you'd move back into the past.

The cylinder Tipler envisaged was so big you wouldn't be able to build it on Earth. It was long enough to span the entire North American continent and heavy enough to sink it like Atlantis. In fact, it needed to be so heavy there was no material on Earth you could use to build it. But there is a material in space – the stuff you find in neutron stars.

Neutron Know-How

Pause here for a brief, worrying look at what happens to stars when they grow old. Stars the size of our sun expand when they start to burn out, frying nearby planets like Mercury, Venus and (gulp) the Earth. But stars that are between two and three times bigger never expand at all. They collapse in on themselves when their fires begin to go out. They get smaller and smaller, more and more dense, until they're not much bigger than a planet. By then they're what's called neutron stars. They're old and cold and the stuff they're made from weighs 1,000,000,000 tonnes a spoonful.

You would need a lot of neutron star stuff to build a Tipler cylinder. In fact, you'd need a lot of neutron stars. Another physicist, Fred Alan Wolf, has calculated that your actual requirement would be around 100 neutron stars. Provided they were spinning at a rate of more than 16,000 kilometres (10,000 miles) a second – which many of them already are – you only need to line them up along their axis of rotation, and you have exactly the type of massive cylinder Tipler envisaged. With your cylinder in place (well outside the solar system), you would have a working time machine.

Frank Tipler's calculations showed that it would produce four zones where space and time were twisted in different ways. Closest to the cylinder itself is the well-named Deadly Zone, where gravity is so great it would rip you apart. Beyond that is the Zone of Time Reversal. Then comes the Null Time Zone, and finally the Zone of Positive Time. Aim your spaceship into the Zone of Time Reversal and you're flying into the past. Aim it into the Zone of Positive Time and you're moving swiftly into the future.

Either way, you can always fly right back

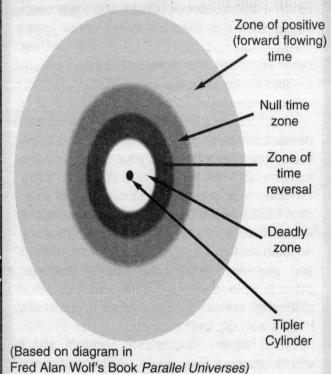

The Cylinder and the Zones

Zone of positive (forward flowing) time

Null time zone

Zone of time reversal

Deadly zone

Tipler Cylinder

(Based on diagram in Fred Alan Wolf's Book *Parallel Universes*)

again. How can this be so? Because it doesn't matter whether it takes us a thousand years, or ten thousand, or ten million years to develop the technology to construct a Tipler cylinder. Once it has been built, it will open gateways which will exist throughout the whole of time. And this means that if it *is* ever built, it's already out there, somewhere in the depths of space, waiting for you now.

When Time gets Tricky

The question is, should you use those gateways if you find them? Time travel involves some very tricky problems that have nothing to do with the technicalities. One of them is illustrated by the Hitler Paradox.

Let's suppose you find time travel easy-peasy. Let's also suppose you've been reading about the Second World War and, being a humane sort of human, you decide you'd like to save the lives of all the people killed in it. Since the Second World War was started by Adolf Hitler, you decide the easiest way to stop it would be to travel back in time before 1939 and push Adolf off a nearby cliff. With Hitler dead, the war will never happen.

Sounds good in theory, but think it through. If you travel back in time and kill Hitler, the war never takes place, so you can never read about it in the history books, so you never travel back in time to kill Hitler, so he does start . . .

And so on, in an endless loop.

You can start to see the problem here. Tinkering with the past can change the future . . . and the future is your present. It doesn't have to be violent tinkering either. Even if you avoid Adolf Hitler, you might accidentally trigger a chain of events with unfortunate conclusions.

Sci-fi writer Ray Bradbury explored this in

'The Sound of Thunder', a short story in which a company called Time Safaris Inc. took clients back to Jurassic times to hunt Tyrannosaurus Rex, the largest of the meat-eating dinosaurs.

The management of Time Safaris were well aware of the dangers of changing the future so they selected a Tyrannosaur that was about to die anyway, crushed by a falling tree, and they provided a levitating metal path so the hunters would not even have to step on to Jurassic earth.

But one of the hunters grew over-excited, jumped off the path and trod on a butterfly. When the party got home again, they discovered their gentle government had been replaced by a violent dictatorship . . . all because of the tiny change made millions of years before.

If the risk of changing the past is so extreme, maybe it would be better to confine our time travelling to the future. Except that could be tricky too. You might, for example, decide to bring back a piece of future technology which would change the world of the present, which would in turn change the future where you found the technology, which would mean . . .

Well, who knows what it would mean? You've just started up another of those paradox loops we came across when we considered time travel into the past. And besides, trips into the future can sometimes produce very nasty surprises. One sci-fi short story tells how the American military, desperate for something to make them invincible against their enemies, arrange for the world's most advanced weapon to be transported back from a period exactly 100 years ahead of their own time. They reckon that, in a century, science would have produced some really stunning guns or bombs.

But when the superweapon of the future finally appears in the transporter, it turns out to be a cross-bow.

Chapter 6

Hi-Tech Fly-Boys

Just two weeks ago, a young scientist made an incredible achievement. He invented a machine that could transport his body from one place to another!

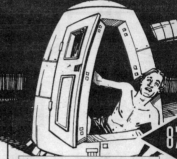

87

He stepped into the first transmitter ...

and appeared, moments later, in the second one!

But since then, he hasn't been feeling himself. He's having weird dreams, his body is changing – and now his skin is coming off in clumps ...

This will change the world!

What's happening to me?

Hi-Tech Fly-Boys

THE FACTS

A particularly gruesome little science-fiction story, *The Fly,* first appeared in an American magazine. But it attracted so much attention that it wasn't long before they made a movie of it starring Vincent Price. That movie proved so popular that they made it again. The remake starred Jeff Goldblum.

The Fly is a simple bedtime tale of a mad scientist obsessed with the idea of matter transmission. Matter transmission is the ultimate way to travel and has been featured endlessly in science fiction. It gets you from here to there (and *there* could be the other side of the world or a distant planet) instantly, without the need for planes, trains or automobiles. It is the concept behind a *Star Trek* transporter system that has carried Away Teams to a multitude of worlds and inspired a T-shirt reading '*Beam me up, Scottie. There's no intelligent life down here.*'

In *The Fly,* the Mad Scientist sets up transmitter and receiver cabinets in his laboratory and sends various bits and pieces from one to the other. After a while, he manages the trick with meat, then with small animals, and he decides the time has come to transport himself. So he climbs into the transmitter and throws the switch.

The way the transmitter works is that it breaks things down into atoms, the tiny building blocks from which everything is made, then it beams the atoms across to the receiver, which puts them back together again. Unfortunately (there's always an 'Unfortunately'), a bluebottle happens to buzz into the transmitter cabinet just as the MS hits the juice, so the two of them get transported at the same time. Even more unfortunately, the receiver gets the two lots of atoms jumbled up when it's putting them together again. Result – poor old MS begins to turn slowly into a fly.

MS's wife watches in helpless horror as he gets more and more hairy and does repulsive insectile things like vomiting up acid from his stomach on to his food before he eats the lot. Since people are a bit slow in movies, she doesn't actually file for divorce until he has developed a monstrous fly's head. And even that isn't the worst of it. The movie ends with her in hysterics because she's just discovered a bluebottle on the window with a little white face that looks just like the MS.

Since there are no flies on the *Enterprise,* this sort of thing doesn't happen in *Star Trek,* where people are beamed all over the place in practically every episode. Chief O'Brien or some other expert energizes, there's a peculiar noise and a shimmering effect and, next thing you know, they're down on the planet without an insect head between them. Geordi LaForge actually tells Lieutenant Barclay in *Star Trek TNG* that

The crew get 'beamed' to another place in Star Trek II: The Wrath of Khan.

transporting is the safest way to travel.

But is it? And is it even possible?

Beaming the bits

The technicalities of matter transmission are frankly daunting. As you sit there reading this book, you are composed of about one hundred thousand billion billion individual atoms – and we are talking British billions here, each one a million million, unlike the US billion, which is only (only!) a thousand million. Each and every one of those atoms fits into a specific place in an almost unbelievably complicated pattern that makes you who and what you are.

You could probably afford to lose an atom or two during matter transmission, but if you lose too many you could end up transmitted minus an arm or some equally important part. If your overall pattern gets scrambled, you could end up transmitted as a boiled egg (admittedly a very *large* boiled egg).

That's why real-life scientists interested in matter transmission don't always think first about transmitting matter (i.e. atoms) at all. They think about transmitting information.

Transmit yourself (just your imagination, not your atoms!) a few years back in time: in the old days, the book you're reading now is written using a typewriter. The finished manuscript – words on paper – is posted off to the publisher. An editor makes a few daft changes, then the manuscript is taken to a printer. The printer gives it to a typesetter operating a Linotype machine. This Lino-operator retypes the entire manuscript on to slugs of hot metal. After the metal has cooled, it is locked into a series of frames, which are used to print the finished book. The type in each frame is inked and paper pressed against it to take up the impression and create the actual pages.

If this sounds unwieldy, it was. It is also a very good example of matter transmission. The matter of the original manuscript was carried to the publisher. The editor made changes on the actual surface of the typescript using something solid like a pen. The all-too-solid matter of the hot-metal slugs was arranged in solid frames and covered with liquid matter in the form of ink so that it could be printed on more matter – the paper that would make up the pages of the finished book.

But if you look carefully, there was an information transfer in there too. When the Lino-operator reset the manuscript, nothing physical passed between the typescript and the hot metal. What was transferred was information.

Nowadays, of course, books are produced very differently – at least by progressive publishers like Puffin. They are written using a computer which stores information as magnetic traces. That information is either sent on a floppy disk or is transferred directly via a modem and phone line to the publisher. The editor makes any necessary changes using a computer – more information transfer – and the text goes on disk to the printer. In the printing works, the old days of hot metal are gone. The information on the disk is transferred to computerized printing machines, which create the pages that are duplicated for the final book.

You can see from this example that sending information is a lot easier than sending matter, which is why fax machines have become our most popular real-life 'matter transmitters'. It's also why the idea of sending just information appeals greatly to those scientists interested in making the *Star Trek* transporter a reality. If you can record all the information about each atom in a human being, then, instead of having to send the atoms themselves, you can simply beam the information and have the person reconstituted from a store of atoms at the far end. You might even modify the Internet to carry the extra traffic.

It's an ingenious solution, but it has its problems. The first of them is fairly murderous: what do you do with the body?

Waste Disposal

If you're beaming me from London to Philadelphia, I come to your transporter station, where I'm scanned and all the information about my atoms is stored on your computer. You then e-mail that info to Philly, where it's used to reconstitute me using local atoms. But since you've sent only the information, not the atoms, I'm still standing in your scanning booth. All you've really succeeded in doing is to create two of me and leave me confused about where I am.

In order to get around that problem, what you need to do is dispose of my body after you've scanned the information but before you've sent it off to Philadelphia. You won't get away with dumping it in the nearest skip. Airlines currently handle several million passengers a year, and your transporter operation might be expected to do even better. Several million bodies would fill up an awful lot of skips. Even if your passengers were agreeable to cremation, the ashes would be enough to bury your whole premises inside a year or two.

What you need is a way to destroy my body completely. The only feasible method of doing this is to convert it into energy. But that also has its problems. Einstein worked out that the amount of energy contained in a given lump of matter can be calculated using the equation $e = mc^2$. The e stands for energy, m for matter and c is the speed of light. Since the speed of light is huge, it will come as no surprise to learn that converting my body into pure energy would have produced an explosion roughly equivalent to

150,000,000,000 tonnes of high explosive – even before I started to put on weight.

And that's just *one* passenger.

Our original idea of beaming the matter itself solves that little problem, but it produces a few new ones.

First, you would need to break my body down to its basic elements. If you go down to the level of the smallest known particle – a quark – that will require about 10 per cent of the energy released when you blew me apart – about 15,000,000,000 tonnes of high explosive – and a temperature about a million times hotter than the sun's core.

But if you go for the cheaper option and break me down only as far as my atoms – which will take a lot less energy – you increase your energy needs when it comes to beaming out the matter stream.

Double Trouble

In order to compete with the airlines, you'll need to manage more or less instantaneous transport like they do in *Star Trek*, and that means a matter stream moving at or about the speed of light. To do that, you'll have to pump in much the same amount of energy as it needed to blow me apart completely when you were trying to get rid of my body.

And you'll still have to send the information stream as well, otherwise Philadelphia won't be able to put me together again at the other end.

Maybe we should just leave matter transmission alone and look to some more manageable visions of the techno-future. After our final Special Section.

Yes … No … Maybe?

The last of our special sections on predictions made ten years ago about technology in the New Millennium

Prediction: Curtainless window

Result: The technology has been around for a long time. Sandwich an LCD (liquid crystal display) panel between two sheets of glass and you've got a window you can black out at the flick of a switch. Are we all using them? Are we heck as like. The problem is: curtains aren't just for privacy. They're for decoration, for keeping the heat in and for peeping around in order to find out what your neighbours are doing. Who would give all that up? A 'No'.

Prediction: Solar-powered torch

Result: This neat little gadget used to sound too daft to be taken seriously. Like, if the sun was shining, you're going to need a torch? But then somebody stopped to think that if the sun – or, better yet, just daylight – charged the batteries, you could use your torch at night. So they made one and it worked and it's here. A 'Yes'.

Prediction: Noise cancellation

Result: Sound moves in waves. If you can generate an equal and opposite wave, it will cancel the first one out. Result: silence. All you need now is a sufficiently powerful dedicated computer that can detect and analyse all the sound waves coming at you and generate their opposites. Presto, you're in a cone of silence. You can't hear your mum telling you to clean your room. You can't hear your dad asking what time do you call this? A New York company was working on it ten years ago, but the Walkman-sized version isn't here yet. I said, THE WALKMAN-SIZED VERSION ISN'T HERE YET!! Soon, 'Maybe'.

Prediction: Water-powered battery

Result: You're probably too young to remember, but they once came up with a clock than ran on potatoes. You stuck a metal spike into the spud and the liquid content generated just enough electricity to power the clock. The water-powered battery was a development of this technology. It uses almost any liquid you choose to pour into it, it's safe, it's cheap and it's environment-friendly. How many have you seen around? Do you think the oil companies had it suppressed? Do you think it was abducted by aliens? Whatever the reason, it's a 'No'.

Prediction: Exercise desk
Result: You know it's not healthy to sit at a desk all day long, whether it's in school or in an office. So the Americans came up with a computer work station that has an exercise bike, treadmill and other wholesome stuff attached. The idea was that you could get on with your work while burning off the calories and keeping yourself fit. Would you buy one? Me neither. Another 'No'.

Prediction: Holographic entertainment
Result: At first the predictions talked about a sort of 3-D TV. Then they moved on to TV in the round using moving versions of those nifty holographic images you can view from any angle. Finally *Star Trek* took it to its ultimate conclusion with the holodeck, where the computer can create any scene and people it with solid holograms you can talk to, kiss or fight.

They're still working to refine the technology. That's a 'Maybe' – and I want one.

∙∙

Prediction: Write-top computers

Result: Another one where the name is a little confusing, but the idea was that sooner or later somebody would develop a computer for people who never learned to type. This machine would be clever enough to recognize your handwriting. That technology has arrived as well – and in little hand-held wonders that you can keep in your pocket. Desktops have gone one further with applications that let you control your computer just by talking to it . . . and dictate letters too. We're doing well: another 'Yes'.

∙∙

Prediction: Intelligent loos

Result: In Japan (where else?) the need was felt for an electrically heated, self-sterilizing loo with a robot arm that would shower your bottom with warm water once you finished your business, dry you off with a blast of hot air, spray you with perfumed mist, then automatically flush when you stood up, playing soft music to you the while. They're big – well, biggish – in Japan; but we British, ever a hardy race, decided there were some things you should do for yourself, and we ignored the invention in our millions. (Although you may come across mechanical self-cleaning loos that revolve, spray and scrub themselves, many people are too wary to use them.) A definite 'No', at least in Britain.

....

Prediction: Smart houses

Result: The idea is: you construct a house that has an integrated communications system, so the lights come on when you enter a room and the TV tells you when your spuds are boiled. Variations on the smart house have been with us for the last few years – one of them lets you call home on your mobile and switch on the oven so that your meal's cooked by the time you arrive. So far they've proved a little too expensive – and maybe even just too scary for the average punter. Make that a 'Maybe'.

....

Prediction: Plastic nails
(no, not fingernails, Doris, *they've* been around for years)

Result: This idea makes *so* much sense. Plastic nails won't rust, they stay three times more firmly in place than metal ones, they literally bond to the surface of the wood, they can be used under water, they won't cause dangerous sparks or wreck power saws and they can be tinted to any colour you need. They were invented years ago. Naturally we've ignored them ever since. A 'No'.

....

Prediction: Microwave clothes drier
Result: We have microwave ovens, so why not microwave clothes driers? They're cheaper to run, don't need outside venting, are easier on your clothes and, since microwaves destroy viruses, they leave things a little healthier all round. So why aren't they selling like hot cakes. Beats me. So far it's another 'No'.

....

Prediction: Electronic pocket organizer
Result: Some time, back in 1989 or 1990, somebody woke up and said: 'Hey, wouldn't it be cool to have a little electronic gadget you could keep in your pocket that would store all your telephone numbers and appointments and memos and stuff like that?' It would and it was and it is, and now everybody has them. Neat prediction. It's a 'Yes'.

....

Prediction: Kiss moisturizer
Result: A dry kiss is no fun (had you noticed?). Which is one reason why Advanced Polymer Systems of California developed micro-sponges, tiny, synthetic, microscopic spheres that can be programmed to deliver moisture in

response to pressure or temperature or even just the passing of a certain amount of time. Microsponges, it was confidently predicted, would one day be incorporated into lipsticks so a girl could renew her colour and keep her lips looking moist and inviting, just by puckering up. The good news is it's here, it's here! They were advertising it on TV last night.

These special sections have been sort of interesting. But when you find the prophets got things wrong, don't laugh too loudly. Remember, every one of these predictions was made inside the last ten years and many were based on technology *already in development*.

What it all adds up to is this: whatever visions sci-fi has about our techno-future, it will be on top of you before you even have time to notice it.

Think Small
THE FACTS

When the evil Borg turned Captain Jean-Luc Picard into one of their own in *Star Trek: The Next Generation,* they used something called nanotechnology.

Nanotechnology is a big word for something small . . . extremely small. What the Borg did was to create robot machines so tiny they could actually be injected into Picard's bloodstream. Once there, they scuttled off and began rebuilding his entire body – effectively changing him into a Borg drone (as members of the Borg Collective are called in the series).

Seven of Nine, the Borg drone who was liberated by Captain Janeway in *Star Trek Voyager,* had her own problems with those little nano-robots. They were so tiny that the

Holographic Doctor could not remove them from her blood. All it took was a dose of radiation and they were activated again, sending Seven racing back to the sinister arms of the Borg Collective.

All this is clearly science fiction. Most scientists will tell you that nanotechnology is strictly Cloud Cuckoo Land, there's no way you could ever build machines so small, and research in the area is a complete waste of money.

But it could be that most scientists are just plain wrong.

One of the cleverest physicists of the twentieth century was a tough-talking New Yorker named Richard Feynman. Coming up to Christmas 1959, Professor Feynman gave a lecture to an audience of three hundred scientists in America. The subject of his talk was making things smaller. In particular, he wanted to explain how it might be possible to write the entire twenty-four volumes of the *Encyclopaedia Britannica* on the head of a pin.

Little Library

During the talk, Feynman told his audience about some calculations he'd made. If you reduced your alphabet to microscopic dots and dashes (like Morse Code) and used it to write text, you could pack all the information in all the world's 24 million books into a cube a quarter of a millimetre (one two-hundredth of an inch) square. That's smaller than a grain of sand. Actually, it's not much bigger than one of those bits of dust you see floating in a sun-beam.

Storing that much information in that little space sounded very far-fetched in 1959, but Feynman reminded his listeners that it had been done already. DNA molecules – which contain the information that makes you what you are – have that sort of storage capacity.

But Feynman's talk wasn't just all about storing information. He suggested it might be possible to go a lot further. He had the idea that one day you would be able to build a machine that would in turn make an exact copy of itself, only smaller – say half size. Then the copy would make another copy, again smaller, and that copy would copy itself small-er still, and so on until you ended up with a machine so tiny it could work with individual atoms.

Once you got down to making things with atoms, all sorts of amazing stuff happened. You could build microscopic machine tools. Then you could use the tiny machine tools to build microscopic factories. And those facto-ries could manufacture computers so small that you wouldn't be able to see them with the naked eye.

The audience spent so much time wondering if Feynman was joking that most of them missed the fact that he was describing a whole new approach to manufacturing.

The way we make things at the moment – and this is the *only* way we make things at the moment – is to take a lump of something and get what we need out of it. The lump could be a block of metal from which we cut a machine part. Or it could be clay from which we make a pot. Or concrete from which we press out blocks. But the basic principle is always the same. We start with a certain quantity of something and whittle it down to size. This is the way we've always done it, right back to the cave days when we chipped flint to make arrowheads.

But what Feynman was talking about wasn't whittling down in any shape or form. He was talking about taking the very smallest lump there was, the basic atom, and using that to build things up. Since everything – including you, your dog, cat, bicycle, TV set, house and lunch-time sandwich – is made from atoms, a machine small enough to handle single atoms could make anything you wanted. Anything at all, from tougher metals and advanced machinery to custom-built animals and plants. You could design new foods, build steaks without killing a single cow, manufacture mushrooms that tasted like kiwi fruit. What you might be able to do by taking this approach was mind-blowing. It would be like starting all over again with the whole of creation.

After he'd talked this way for an hour, Feynman did something that was really dumb for such a clever man. He announced that, in order to encourage people to think from this new viewpoint, he was going to offer two prizes of $1,000 each. The first was to go to anybody who could show it really *was* possible to write the *Encyclopaedia Britannica* on the head of a pin. They didn't have to write the whole encyclopaedia. All they had to do was take a page from a book and write it 25,000 times smaller, which was the scale you'd need to do the *Britannica* trick. Oh yes, and it would still have to be readable – even though you might need an electron microscope to read it. Why an electron microscope? Because when you're looking at something *really* small, you can't use light, because light particles are big enough to knock it over. So instead you use electrons, which are smaller. An electron microscope lets you look at things that are too small to be seen when there's light around.

The second prize was even more straightforward. It would go to the first person who made a working electric motor that could fit into a cube measuring four-tenths of a millimetre (one sixty-fourth of an inch) in all directions.

The reason why this announcement was really dumb was because Feynman didn't have

$2,000 to give away. He didn't even have $1,000. But he wasn't worried because he was convinced it couldn't be done – not in his lifetime at least. He thought his money was safe.

He was wrong.

In the year after he announced his competition, Feynman had plenty of entries, but nothing he saw came anywhere near fitting into a cube measuring four-tenths of a millimetre.

Then, in November 1960, a young man named Bill McLellan walked into the office carrying a box. But he didn't take a little motor out of the box. He took out a microscope. He looked Feynman in the eye and explained that the McLellan motor was so small you needed a microscope to see it.

You did too. The motor used insulated wire that was just one hundredth of a millimetre (one two-thousandth of an inch) thick. It was wound around four tiny iron pins. Inserted between them was a miniature magnetized disc attached to a near-invisible metal shaft. What with bearings and other bits and pieces, the whole thing had thirteen separate parts. It weighed 250 micrograms (that's less than four thousandths of a grain – and there are 437.5 grains in an ounce!) and it fitted into a cube measuring four-tenths of a millimetre. When you looked through the microscope and turned on the electricity, you could see the drive shaft spinning at anything up to 2,000 revs per minute in complete silence. The whole thing was so small it didn't produce enough energy to make a noise.

McLellan had to wait several days for his prize, because it took Feynman that long to raise the money. Fortunately it was nearly 25 years before he had to pay out on the second one. But pay out he did.

Getting Even Smaller

Some people never learn, even people of genius. In 1983 Professor Feynman gave another talk to scientists about making things small. He had Bill McLellan's little motor with him and astonished his audience by remarking that in the twenty-four years since he gave his first talk, science had moved so far ahead that it was now possible – even easy – to build a motor 64,000 times smaller. He thought machines that small could be great for a new type of computer game. You built one in the shape of a little man, gave it a sword and dropped it in the water with a paramecium. (A paramecium is a real-life microscopic monster no larger than a single cell.) Then you watched through a microscope to see who'd win the fight.

After the talk, a student at America's Stanford University named Tom Newman decided to try reducing the *Encyclopaedia*

Britannica to fit on the head of a pin. He did a few calculations to find out just how small it would have to be. The answer was frightening. To write text that small, each letter would have to be no more than fifty atoms wide.

It's almost impossible to imagine a width of fifty atoms, but Newman created a computer program to etch the first page of *A Tale of Two Cities* by Charles Dickens. It took just one minute to do the job and prove that *Britannica* could fit on a pinhead. Newman claimed the prize. It was the fastest $1,000 he ever earned.

But even though it was beginning to look as if there might be something in Feynman's idea of building very small machines, most scientists could not work up any enthusiasm for it. One problem was, they couldn't think what use the machines would be. Writing *A Tale of Two Cities* on a pinhead might be impressive, but it didn't actually *do* anything.

Juggling with Jiggles

Another problem was this: if you take a glass of water, or any other liquid, and look at it under a really powerful microscope, you'll find the molecules jiggle about all the time. This happens because jiggling is the way heat shows up when you're working on that tiny scale.

Since absolutely everything that we find

useful contains a certain amount of heat, everything that we find useful has molecules that jiggle. Molecules are usually a bit bigger than atoms. But when you go down to atomic size or below, the situation is even more complicated. Once you reach that scale, it's nearly impossible to measure where a particle is at any particular time.

You can see right away why this would put scientists off thinking about building bulldozers and forklifts small enough to shunt single atoms around. If you can't even find the things you're supposed to be working with, and anyway they're jumping about all over the place when you do find them, it's hard to figure out how you could ever use them as building blocks.

But while most scientists were convinced that all this ruled out nanotechnology as a practical science, there was one who was thinking very differently.

Eric Drexler seems to have been born interested in the world of the very, very small. He was little more than a toddler when Richard Feynman delivered his first talk on the subject but, even without hearing what Feynman had to say, Drexler managed to turn the whole subject into a lifelong obsession.

What really triggered his interest was when his professors at the Massachusetts Institute of Technology taught him about *genetic* engineering. Genetic engineering is big news nowadays. Genes are the blueprints that make all living things (including you) grow to be the way they are. By changing a gene here and there, you can make a huge difference to the finished product. You can create tomatoes that stay fresh longer. You can grow a human ear on the back of a mouse (it's been done). You can also cure a great many illnesses.

But that's now. Back when Drexler was a student, genetic engineering was in a start-up situation. There was a lot more theory than practice. The new breed of genetic engineer was thinking about changing the genes of a simple virus so that it would produce the insulin diabetics need, or drugs or vaccines.

When Drexler learned how genetic engineering worked, he began to wonder why you had to stop with things like insulin or vaccines. What was to stop you using genetic engineering to grow something *really* useful . . . like a tiny computer? You'll remember that Richard Feynman had the same idea in 1959, but Drexler hadn't read Feynman's talk at this time. He got to the same place all on his own. And while Feynman stopped at the basic idea, Drexler started thinking how you might actually do it.

The ideas he came up with were like nothing anybody had ever dreamed about before. It struck him that it would make sense to build his tiny computer with the materials already available in nature. He was still thinking like a genetic engineer, so he had a picture of a computer made out of proteins and lipids and other things you find in living creatures. But the computer wouldn't be a living creature. It would be a machine made out of living tissue.

But by 1977 Drexler was edging away from the idea of making a tiny computer. That sort of machine would be useful anywhere you needed to control a really small engine – like a cancer cure that worked directly on the cells – but he could think of other devices that would be even more useful. One would be a piece of molecular machinery that was small enough to manipulate molecules to build better molecular machinery. If the second generation of molecular machines was better than the first, they in turn could build third-generation machines that were better than themselves. If you continued this process, pretty soon you would have very efficient little machines indeed. It's the same principle as computers that are now building more intelligent computers.

Endless Possibilities?

As he approached the end of his student days, Drexler was seized by a vision. If you could create the basic machinery to stack one molecule on top of another, maybe even shove single atoms around, then you could literally manufacture anything that it was physically possible to create. You could set up a factory that could fabricate materials stronger than steel and lighter than feathers. Or turn out apples that tasted like oranges. Or build yourself a kitten that would never grow up into a cat.

Once nano-factories went into production, you could turn the atoms and molecules of rubbish tips into nourishing and delicious food. Or fuel to keep you warm and run your car. You could wipe out global poverty and hunger for ever. You could create a world in which we could all have as much as we wanted of anything we wanted. There were no limits at all to what you could do. Nanotechnology could turn humanity into a race of gods.

And objects like computer chips were definitely getting smaller and smaller. Maybe it only needed somebody to spell out the possibilities, and science would really get down to the nano level. Drexler came to much the same conclusion as Feynman. He decided to share his vision of tiny machines.

To this end he started work on a book entitled *Engines of Creation*. It was an engineer's examination of what nanotechnology could do and a discussion of the effect it might have on the world we live in.

The Negative Side of Nano

As Drexler wrote, it became clear that nanotechnology wasn't all a bowl of cherries. Unlimited supplies of everything you need or want at next to no cost sounds like getting the keys to the sweet shop. But what happens to all the existing factories and the people who work in them? What happens to your national economy?

And nanotechnology wasn't just about manufacturing goodies. With the right nanomachines you could repair any damage suffered by the human body. You could cure every disease. You could fix the effects of ageing. There was actually a fighting chance that you might help people to live for ever – or at least for several hundred years.

That wasn't all good news either. If people started living for several hundred years, the world would get extremely overcrowded very quickly. To fix this, you would have to limit the birth rate. Then children would become a rarity. So would new ideas, new fashions, new ways of thinking about things since, whether we realize it or not, new ideas are brought into society mainly by new (i.e. young) people.

Even aside from that little problem, what would people *do*? With everything they could ever want at their fingertips, they certainly wouldn't have to work. Entertainment would be limited because entertainers wouldn't have to work either. How on earth would people fill their days?

These are not easy problems, and it would be a lot better if we began thinking about them *before* the nano-factories start up rather than waiting until the crisis is upon us. But, now Drexler put his mind to it, he realized there weren't just *problems* with nanotechnology, there were *risks* as well.

One of those risks was a horror worse than all the disaster movies put together.

This risk arises out of a single, simple fact. Building just one nano-machine gets you absolutely nowhere. Even if it's a perfect little assembler that can shove individual atoms anywhere it likes, it could work away for a million years and you still wouldn't see the result. The change one nano-machine can make to the world is just too small.

To get around this, the experts have suggested that nano-machines need to be able to reproduce themselves. They have to be able to make copies of themselves before they start making anything else. Why? Because while one nano-machine won't make much difference to anything, a few thousand billion of them might be capable of building you a car.

But suppose the reproduction process got out of hand . . .

When one tiny machine builds a copy of

itself, it uses the raw materials – the atoms and molecules – it finds around it. In other words, it uses tiny pieces of the physical world; it eats them up to create the duplicate. That's absolutely fine if you're building a few thousand copies or even a few million. At the scale we're talking about, a single pebble you picked up on the beach could keep the nano-machines going for centuries.

But once you stop to do the maths involved in self-replicating nano-machines, machines that are designed to reproduce themselves, the picture that comes up is positively terrifying. Here's how it goes:

You take maybe ten or twenty years building your very first nano-machine, getting it absolutely perfect, ironing out the bugs. Then you set it running.

The first thing your new machine does is to build a copy of itself. This won't take another twenty years, of course, or anything like. It will probably take a little over fifteen minutes.

Then the two machines – your original and the copy – each start copying themselves. In half an hour from the time you started, you will have four neat little assemblers all grafting away to make copies of themselves. In an hour, your original assembler has turned into sixteen nano-machines.

Nothing very scary about that, but keep doing the sums. In ten hours you have a swarm of more than 68,000,000,000 nano-machines on your hands and every one of them is hell-bent on copying itself, using any atoms it finds in the world around it.

Of course, as a good nano-engineer you will have designed those machines to stop reproducing once they reach a certain point. But if you've ever worked a machine you'll know that sooner or later something will go wrong. If the safeguards you've built into your nano-assemblers go wrong at any time, this is what will happen.

The 'Gray Goo' Effect

Inside a day you will have so many nano-machines that you will be able to weigh them. They will weigh more than a ton. The atoms they used to duplicate themselves will have left a gaping hole in your laboratory.

But that's nothing compared to what's coming next. In less than two days, your machines will have eaten your home, your family, friends and yourself (since people too are made from atoms), your street, your town, your country and, indeed, the entire planet. Everything, but everything, on Earth will have turned into hungry little replicating machines.

In another four hours they will have eaten the whole of the solar system.

Let me run that by you one more time. If the

fail-safes you have built into your design break down at any time in just one single nano-machine, it will EAT THE ENTIRE SOLAR SYSTEM WITHIN FORTY-EIGHT HOURS.

Drexler called this the 'gray goo effect'. Runaway nanotechnology could turn the whole universe into a 'gray goo' (something resembling porridge, I suppose) of tiny machines that do nothing but try to reproduce themselves.

Today, young Eric Drexler is *Doctor* Eric Drexler, a respected scientist and engineer who has lost none of his enthusiasm for nanotechnology despite its potential to eat the world. He reckons that you might be able to stop a runaway gray goo effect by creating nano-machines that are designed to destroy the rogue assemblers that keep on reproducing. It's an idea he borrowed from nature; your blood contains white cells which fight invading bacteria and viruses in just this way.

You'd better hope he is right, because nanotechnology is definitely edging closer.

A scientist named Hans Dehmelt has solved the problem, mentioned earlier, of finding particles and keeping molecules from jiggling. He devised a laser trap that can isolate and hold a single particle; so manipulating atoms and molecules is now, just as Drexler predicted, no more than an engineering problem.

Two European scientists, Gerd Binnig and Heinrich Rohrer, became the first people on

Earth to move single atoms about. They did it accidentally – they were working on something else at the time – but since then other scientists have moved atoms on purpose. In the Research Division of IBM in California there is now a company logo and a map of the world picked out in single atoms.

So how long will it be before we have nano-machines capable of taking over Jean-Luc Picard, manufacturing everything you've ever wanted and eating up the world if they go wrong? Senator Al Gore, who later became Vice-President of the United States, once put just that question to the expert, Dr Eric Drexler.

Drexler thought it over carefully, then told Gore that, from the day you find the money for the research, the whole thing should be up and running inside fifteen years.

Your Techno Future

Not even the experts (especially the experts!) can be sure how new technology will change our lives. But if it keeps on developing as it has been over the last century, one thing's sure – the next millennium will bring a whole new world. Think of all the inventions a ninety-year-old person living today has seen: the radio, TV, telephone, the Internet ... it just goes on and on. Now imagine technology developing as fast as that in the next ninety years – in **your** lifetime! Think what that might bring! But whether you're headed for the stars or living in a virtual world, your techno future's going to be fun.

Unless you're eaten up by gray goo, of course.

Who's Who in the Particle Zoo?

These days physicists work with so many tiny bits of matter it would make your head spin. Some are so small they're no longer really matter, but a cross between matter and energy. Others are so small they aren't really there at all. Most can't be seen directly by any means at all. Scientists know they're there because they leave trails in a specially prepared space called a bubble chamber. The list that follows will introduce you to just a very few of the pieces that go to make up your world . . . and you.

Molecules
These are the smallest bits of anything that still have the same properties as the original. If you come across a hydrogen gas molecule, for example, you can tell at once that it came from hydrogen and not from oxygen or a lump of aluminium.

Atoms
The ancient Greeks thought the world must be

made up of little bits of matter. My teacher, who wasn't an ancient Greek, explained that if you took a brick and chopped it in half, then took one of the halves and chopped that in half and kept doing that for a very long time you would eventually end up with a bit of brick so small you couldn't split it any more. That tiny, tiny bit of brick was an atom. Then, in 1932, a couple of Cambridge physicists *did* split it. So now you have to say that an atom is the smallest bit you can chop the brick into without things called 'charged particles' being released.

Particles

Particles are little things you find inside an atom, and they're designed to drive you nuts. Imagine them as tiny cannonballs – as physicists did for years – and you'd be right. Imagine them as tiny waves of energy and you'd also be right! Don't tell me that doesn't make sense: I have troubles of my own.

Electrons

Electrons are one kind of particle you might find if you cracked open an atom. Rivers of electrons running through wires are what we call electricity.

Photons

There are several billion photons hitting you in

the eye as you read this. Photons are particles of light. I can never understand why *Star Trek*'s photon torpedoes do any more damage to a Klingon warbird than shining an electric torch at it would.

Muons

These are particles that travel very fast, up there close to the speed of light. At that speed, time changes pace. So if we could use muons to power a spaceship, we would age about seven times less on the journey than the time it took us to get there, thus deeply confusing our mother. Fortunately we don't know how to build a muon-powered spaceship, so it doesn't really matter.

Tachyons

These souped-up particles travel faster than light and thus go backwards in time. (At light speed, time stops. Faster than light speed, it goes into reverse.) We've spotted their trails in a bubble chamber, but we haven't caught one yet, probably because we're whizzing forward in time while they're whizzing backwards.

Neutrinos

There's so little to these particles that most of them pass right through our entire planet without even noticing that it is there. People ridiculed the physicist Wolfgang Pauli when he predicted that neutrinos would be discovered, but he had the last laugh when they were. These are the ones that ghosts would be made of – if you believed in ghosts.

Quarks

The even smaller particles that make up the tiny particles we've been looking at above. Physicists hope and pray quarks are as small as particles are going to get, but personally I wouldn't bank on it.

Quark's

The bar on *Deep Space Nine* that is run by everybody's favourite Ferengi.

Glossary

AI Stands for Artifical Intelligence – intelligence created by humans, usually meaning machines that give the impression of being intelligent.

android A machine made to talk, act and look like a human.

atomic clock A super-accurate timepiece driven by radioactive material.

avatar An icon or photograph that represents you on an Internet chat site.

bit The smallest piece of information a computer can handle.

black hole A region in space where gravity is so strong, not even light can escape. Nearby matter is pulled into it.

byte 8 bits (see above).

a console Set of controls for electronic equipment.

cosmic radiation Rays of energy from outer space beaming around the universe.

cyberspace The world that is created by multi-millions of computers all hooked on to the Internet.

database A collection of information held in a structured way on a computer.

digital When numbers are used to represent tiny pieces of information in an electronic device.

DNA Deoxyribonucleic acid, molecule which carries the information, in very long code, that tells your body how to work. It is essential for life as we know it.

evolution A gradual change in the characteristics of animal or plants over many generations, so that they adapt in the best way to survive.

futurologist Someone who forecasts the future based on current trends.

gene A unit made up of DNA (see above) that enables a living thing to pass on characteristics to the next generation. The science of manipulating genes is called genetic engineering.

gravity The force that gives things weight by pulling them towards a mass of matter.

hardware The physical parts of a

computer system eg monitor, printer, keyboard, mouse.

humanoid Something which is like a human being.

hydraulically-operated Run by liquid moving in a confined space under pressure.

IBM Stands for International Business Machines, the largest computer company in the world.

imprinting The instinct many newborn animals have to attach themselves emotionally to the first thing they see, usually their mothers.

infrared A type of light emitted by something hot like the sun. We cannot see it with our bare eyes.

instinct A natural impulse.

interface Something that connects a computer to a person so that they can interact, for example a mouse, a keyboard, an icon.

intuition When you know or feel something by instinct, not by reason or logic.

IQ Stands for Intelligence Quotient. This is a measurement of human intelligence made by a special test.

kilobyte 1024 bytes (See above).

laser Stands for Light Amplification by Stimulated Emission of Radiation. A device that gives off photons to make an intense beam of very strong light. It can be used for example in drilling, cutting and surgery.

matter transmission Moving something from one place to another. This could be information sent, for example, via a fax machine. In science fiction, it is a method of instant transportation. Matter is broken down into individual atoms so that it can be beamed elsewhere and reassembled.

130

microchip A tiny wafer of silicon which contains miniature electric circuits that can store millions of bits of information.

modem Comes from two words: MOdulation and DEModulation. A device that connects two computers together over a telephone line by converting the computer's data into an audio signal.

nanotechnology The science that explores manipulating individual atoms and molecules, therefore working on a minute scale.

neutron star A very old, cold, extremely dense, burnt-out star, mainly composed of neutrons.

paradox A statement which seems to contradict itself but is surprisingly saying something true.

patent The sole right, granted by the government to an inventor to manufacture, use or sell an invention.

positronic brain A fictional robot brain invented by Dr Isaac Asimov and taken up by other sci-fi writers.

prophet A person who claims to be able to say what will happen in the future.

prototype The first model of a particular type of machine, on which other forms are then based.

robot An automatically operated machine that does the work a human used to do.

satellite Something that revolves around a planet. Nowadays artificial satellites are often used for communications.

sensor A mechanical device sensitive to things like light, temperature or radiation level, that transmits a signal to a measuring or control instrument.

smart card A card with a built-in computer chip that allows it to store information, activate machinery, etc.

software A set of instructions that tell your computer what to do, making it useful to you, eg Office, games, web browsers.

solar system A group of planets orbiting a star. Our solar system is made up of nine planets which orbit our star, the Sun.

universe Everything in space, including all galaxies, stars and planets.

virtual reality When a computer makes you believe you are in a different situation or environment by using for example a helmet, earphones and goggles.

virus In humans and animals, a virus is something that spreads infection and makes us ill. In computers, a virus is a programme which can damage the files on your PC. It is often intentionally created to do damage, and spreads secretly via shared disks and telephone lines.

wireheading A theoretical method of having a computer chip put inside your brain so that you can experience ultimate virtual reality, without the goggles, helmet and earphones.

Index

133

135